What Becomes *of the* Brokenhearted

Michelle McKinney Hammond

HARVEST HOUSE
PUBLISHERS
Eugene, Oregon 97402

Cover by Koechel Peterson & Associates, Minneapolis, Minnesota

Published in association with the literary agency of Alive Communications, Inc., 7680 Goddard Street. Ste #200, Colorado Springs, CO 80920

WHAT BECOMES OF THE BROKENHEARTED
Copyright © 2001 by Michelle McKinney Hammond
Published by Harvest House Publishers
Eugene, Oregon 97402

Library of Congress Cataloging-in-Publication Data
McKinney Hammond, Michelle, 1957–
    What becomes of the brokenhearted / Michelle McKinney Hammond.
      p. cm.
    ISBN 0-7369-0527-8
    1. Consolation. I. Title.
    BV4905.3 M35 2001
    248.8'6 —dc21   00-046122

Printed in the United States of America

02 03 04 05 06 / BP-CF / 10 9 8 7 6 5 4 3

To my Heavenly Father, my Divine Protector
My Lord and Savior, consuming Lover of my Soul
Precious Holy Spirit—my Comforter, my Guide.

For all the brokenhearted who long for relief
and the assurance that they will live and love again.

For all who choose to embrace the spirit of survival.

For all those who feel too weak to begin again. But will.

For those who are afraid to try again, but
more afraid of giving up.

This is for all of you. I feel you. And He does too.

Acknowledgments

To my Harvest House family. I love you more with each book that I write. Thank you for your sweet and special spirits. Your support has pulled things out of me that I did not think were possible. You are an inspiration and a jewel. You make my work a joy!

To my inner core, who keep me strong through mentorship, accountability, prayer, and sound counsel. I love you all. You know who you are. Don't stop telling me the truth, even when I don't like it.

Valencia, thank you for your constant assistance. I love and appreciate you. You are a gift I don't take for granted.

Nicole, thanks for making me look good on paper and for keeping me focused. I love you, my sister.

Cindy, thanks for always listening to me, even when you're sleepy (smile).

Chip, you really *are* the best agent in the whole world.

Contents

Let's Get Free! ⌒ 7

1. Ouch! ⌒ 13

2. Adam, Where Art Thou? ⌒ 29

3. Hell Hath No Fury… ⌒ 45

4. Under the Juniper Tree ⌒ 63

5. Coming Clean ⌒ 83

6. Balloons in the Wind ⌒ 99

7. Rebuilding the Temple ⌒ 119

8. The Woman in the Mirror ⌒ 135

9. Embracing the Altar ⌒ 155

10. Facing Tomorrow ⌒ 173

Let's Get Free!

So here we are. You are hurting, and I can relate. Been there. Done that. Unfortunately, we will do it again if the process of healing is not allowed to do its work. It is time not only to decide to live but also to learn from our trials. The biggest mistake I've ever made is to sweep my tears under a rug, square my shoulders, and move on, stumbling blindly over my disappointments only to find myself staring them in the face at a later date that was not so convenient. For every lesson I refused to learn, every heartache I refused to process, the backlash was worse than the original occurrence. All of my secret pain only compelled me to sabotage new possibilities. This is why I'm glad you are reading this now. I hope that my lessons will become your lessons and save you more grief than what you are presently experiencing.

But I must warn you that healing takes work. You must be willing to do it. Healing usually hurts in the beginning. But it will only hurt for as long as you fight the medicine. So open wide. Let's get real. Let's get honest. But most of all, let's get free! Forget about the other person. This is all about you. So get ready to dig deep. We are going to get rid of everything that impedes your progress toward a new day. Out with stinking thinking and self-destructive conduct. Pull up a chair. Get real comfortable. Grab your pen and pad. We're going to work this thing out together. We're going to talk and write. Then we'll take a look at what you've written and separate the sense from the nonsense. We're going to take responsibility for our hearts. We're going to get it right this time. Get ready to exhale *and* inhale. A new breath. The breath of life! We're going to discover the ability to celebrate love all over again. Oooh, I'm excited! Aren't you?!

Michelle

What becomes of the brokenhearted
   left to groan
      at the travesty of affliction and abandonment
   left to grieve over shattered tomorrows
is there any hope?
   or will they forever
      be tossed by the tempest of disappointment
   disillusionment
      and despair?
   where does their help come from?
to whom can they turn
   in the wake of fearing to trust and love again?
  can shattered pieces be mended?
      or will they forever lie in disrepair?
   these are the questions
      of those that mourn
   but surely hearts that are broken will beat again
      loud and strong
         as they yield to healing hands
            that bind the wounded places
         acknowledging their pain
         and soothing them
            with the ointment of promises
            rich and true

yes, there is a ray of light
that brings a resounding faith in tomorrow
as it rises over the mountain of doubt
that separates the Son
from the forsaken
it comes in answer to whispered prayers
barely audible
for the strength to utter them has been depleted
and yet the Son hears and comes
bearing healing and light
comfort and relief
replacing weeping with laughter
mourning with joy
in the morning after the darkness passes
spring comes where tears have been spent
leaving fruitful blooms to thrive
and feed those who will follow
the path to wholeness
for those who say yes to the climb
shall be restored
to live and love again

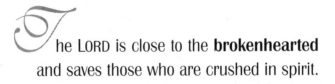

The LORD is close to the **brokenhearted**
and saves those who are crushed in spirit.

Psalm 34:18, emphasis mine

1

Ouch!

As I stood at the top of the waterslide looking down, I could feel the excitement, the expectation of an incredible experience. I carefully settled onto the mat, awaiting my moment to push off. The sky was an incredible shade of blue. The sun looked brilliant. It reflected off the droplets of water that danced through the air as laughing children effortlessly rode the descending cascade, leaving swirls of water kissing the air behind them. Yes, it was a perfect day for embracing the wind.

I took a deep breath and abandoned myself to the rushing breezes that were playing tag with my hair. It was so exhilarating! I felt the blood rush to my cheeks. My heart pounded in my ears. I felt so free! I threw back my head, laughing to release the joy I felt coursing through my being. And then it happened. As I sailed over the last hump of this wonderful ride, my mat flew out and straight ahead into the air, leaving the slide completely. I hung suspended in mid-flight for the smallest moment before gravity harshly brought me back down to earth. *Bam!* My landing took my breath away—literally. Pain ran up my spine. I felt nauseated. I fought to breathe, but my lungs, bewildered by the sudden expulsion of oxygen, didn't know how to respond.

Daddy said that I turned green as my eyes sought him out in the crowd, pleading for him to rescue me from my agony. As he came to me and gently lifted me to carry me to safer ground, I felt comforted but none the better for the rest of the afternoon. The happy squeals of those who had not suffered as I had faded in my ears as I left the park grounds. My back hurt for several days and the memory of my misadventure stung every time I recollected it. I had not only been hurt physically, I was also wounded emotionally—I was embarrassed. Why had I been unable to master something that others so effortlessly enjoyed? Needless to say, to this day I have never returned for another round of water fun.

As I recall my first heartbreak, I realize that my feelings following it were quite similar to how I felt that day at the water park. I was caught off-guard. I had settled in to enjoy the elation of love only to find my heart suddenly grounded. The wind was knocked out of my sails. The shame, the pain, nauseated and paralyzed me. I sat looking bewildered. I was much older now, no longer small enough or light enough for my daddy to pick me up and carry me away from the scene of the devastation, but I longed for comfort just the same. And this wasn't just a ride. This was my life, and it really hurt! The solution was not as simple as spanking the side of the slide and saying, "Bad ride!" This situation was a lot more complex. Would I recover? How long would it take for my heart to stop stinging? Would I ever be able to breathe again? Laugh again? See others enjoying the ride of love without wanting to cry? At the time I had no answers, but I have them now.

If you've ever pondered the same questions or had the same experience, then you've come to the right place. Does anyone relate to your pain? Oh, yes. But more importantly, the only One who can do something about your suffering is also well-acquainted with heartbreak. As a matter of fact, He was the first to experience it. God's hands lovingly molded Adam and his counterpart, Eve. The Lord gave them His all. He gave them Himself. Right down to His very breath. And yet they turned from Him to become masters of their own lives. They preferred to indulge themselves in the lust of the flesh, the lust of the eyes, and the pride of life rather than revel in His unselfish care. The breath He shared with them, the breath that linked them together with Him and made the three— Father, man, and woman—one, was rejected. The three-fold cord was broken. Severed by their disobedience, God felt rejected. Betrayed. God was heartbroken.

> "I will **never leave** you nor forsake you" (Joshua 1:5, emphasis mine).

> "I have loved you with an **everlasting love**; I have drawn you with loving-kindness" (Jeremiah 31:3, emphasis mine).

These are the words we all long to hear, yet there is only One who cannot—no! *will not*—lie or deceive. There is only One who will never break His promises. That is

God, and God alone. Yet more often than not, He is not the one to whom we entrust our hearts for safekeeping. In our search for immediate gratification, we offer our hearts to those who seem to offer us tangible love. We, like Adam and Eve, snatch our hearts out of God's hands, eager to give up our trust in Him for a seemingly more attractive prize. Too many times we find ourselves gazing in despair at the shattered fragments of our hearts as the one to whom we entrusted our love drops or damages this most important treasure.

Will the pain ever end? Yes, it will. I can say that with great assurance. However, the process of healing takes time. Ironic, isn't it? In our quest for instant fulfillment, we find ourselves still forced to learn the lesson of patience. How long will the process of mending take? That depends on the depth of the wound and your willingness to embrace each step toward your wholeness.

Taking Things to Heart

The wind of heartbreak blows from many directions. It is a cold gust that chills our souls to the bone, no matter what the offense against us. Rejection, betrayal, violation, deceit, loss—it doesn't matter what form the disappointment takes; the effects can change our entire life. This is why God tells us that the state of our heart is a matter of life and death. It affects the quality of our lives on a daily basis.

> "Above all else, **guard** your **heart**, for it is the wellspring of life" (Proverbs 4:23, emphasis mine).

> "**Hope deferred** makes the heart sick, but a longing fulfilled is a tree of life" (Proverbs 13:12, emphasis mine).

So, your heart has been broken. Still, there is hope for you. Healing awaits you. It is within your reach, depending on the choices you make. The world says that the best revenge is success. Though it is not revenge that you should be seeking, this saying has a grain of truth if you emerge from your present circumstances as a better, stronger you. God has His own way of dealing with those who hurt us as we focus on the only person we have control over—ourselves.

As I looked through Scripture at those who had also encountered heartbreak, I was struck by what a difference attitude can make in the outcome of an encounter with unwelcome pain. There is a lot we can learn from these stories to help us in our own quest for recovery. Can one bounce back from cruel rejection, inexcusable betrayal, devastating loss, even the violation of one's body, heart, and soul? Yes, yes, yes! Others have, and you will too. As you join me on this path, we are going to follow others who have been before us.

Let's consider Joseph, who was sold into slavery by his own brothers. They say that only those close to you can truly hurt you, and though we know this to be true, no one accepts the reality of it until it happens. Can you imagine how Joseph felt as he was led down the dusty road to Egypt? How many times do you think he looked backward down the path hoping against hope that he would see his brothers coming to reverse what they had done? And yet they didn't come. Consider the days he worked as a slave in Potiphar's house. This young man who had been his father's favorite, who had reaped all the perks that favoritism brings, had been reduced to serving as a slave in a stranger's house! Can you for one moment think of the questions he had for God? I can! Oh, and let's not speak of the further injury added to insult when Potiphar's wife then accused Joseph of trying to rape her because he refused to sleep with her. He was thrown in jail even though he was innocent. From the young age of seventeen to the ripe maturity of forty, there was much that occurred in Joseph's life that could have caused him to grow bitter and question the existence and fairness of God.

Yet in spite of all of this, Joseph clung to God, and God turned his situation around. Joseph rose to prominence in Egyptian society, becoming the right-hand man of the Pharaoh himself. He died a wealthy man, with the saving of a nation to his credit, surrounded by all that he desired. He said it best when he named his children Manasseh, which meant, "God has caused me to forget all my troubles and all my father's house," and Ephraim, which meant, "God has made me fruitful in the land of my affliction" (Genesis 41:51-52). In essence, God replaced everything that Joseph had been "robbed" of—and more. He was restored to his family, and he greeted them with joy and forgiveness. Joseph chose to glean a valuable insight from all that he suffered over the natural inclination to become bitter and vengeful.

> "You intended to harm me, but God intended it for good to accomplish what is now being done, the saving of many lives" (Genesis 50:20).

We should be able to celebrate some level of higher learning from all that we go through, and yet some of us do not do this. Some of us remain in a state of desolation after we have been scarred. Such was the case with Tamar, the daughter of king David who was raped by her brother Amnon. Amnon thought himself sick with love. Longing and pining for Tamar reduced him to a deep depression.

Through the encouragement of a wily cousin, he lured Tamar to his room under the guise of seeking a healing dish from her hands. And there he violated not only her body but her spirit as well, leaving her a broken woman. In a society that valued virginity, she was now considered undesirable. Discarded. She lived the rest of her days in the house of her brother Absalom, devastated and reliving over and over again the violence wrought against her. Though Absalom avenged her by killing Amnon, there was no justice that could restore the woman she used to be. Covered by shame and despair, Tamar lived out her remaining days in darkness. She died a little more inside each day until death mercifully rescued her.

No one should accept such a fate as Tamar's. To become among the walking dead is needless and unfair to those who love you. Imagine their grief and sense of failure when you resign from life. Going inside yourself and remaining in the hidden chambers of your own pain is exactly what the enemy of your soul wants you to do. Don't give him that satisfaction. Choose life over death, joy over sorrow. The power to make these choices is in your hands. You are just a thought, just a word, just a step away from all of your tomorrows. You must decide what their outcome will be.

Getting to the Heart of the Matter

Like the Shunammite woman who refused to accept the death of her only son, we must fiercely choose to snatch that which we have termed lost back from the jaws of death. Jesus has given us this power.

> "Where, O **death**, is your victory? Where, O **death**, is your **sting**?" (1 Corinthians 15:55, emphasis mine).

As the Shunammite woman held her dead son in her arms, all she knew was that she could not allow life to come to this. Gently laying her son down on the prophet's bed, she dressed herself and went in search of Elisha, this prophet who had prophesied the birth of the child she had long given up hope of having. And yet her son had been born within the year, just as Elisha had said. No, she would not give him up now! God was not a cruel jester, playing tricks of this sort. "It's not over until it's over," she said under her breath as she climbed atop her donkey. And each person whom she passed heard the same reply as they asked her how she fared. "All is well," she said. "All is well." And so it was. She did not stop until she finally saw the prophet in the distance. Only to him would she voice her predicament. After all, he had started this. He and God were the only responsible parties. Only they could fix it. All the way back to the house, with the prophet beside her, she held her same confession. All is well. Later, cradling her son in her arms—the son brought back to life by the man of God—she hummed as she stroked his brow, "All is well."

All is well because all *must* be well if God is involved. As Jesus hung dying on the cross, He looked at those who had scorned and rejected Him. Abused Him and cursed Him. His gaze also took notice of those not present in the crowd. Those who had sold Him out, betrayed Him, lied to Him, disowned and abandoned Him. Still, He knew that "all is well." He saw the other side of His situation. He knew the reward for His suffering. He did not take what had happened personally. He knew the weaknesses of His offenders, and He pitied them. After all, their suffering was greater than His, and it would continue long after He claimed the victory. He embraced His pain and saw its value.

This was a lesson Samson learned even after being over-powered by his own bad choices. He finally saw in the darkness what he should have seen in the light. He reflected on all that he had lost and finally learned the lessons his pain sought to teach him. The woman Samson loved had told his secrets and exposed his vulnerabilities to those who did not have his best interest at heart. He had given himself freely to a woman who was calculating and hardened, who exchanged his affections for tangible reward, something she could use even as she had used him. Betrayal of this nature cuts to the core of our being, and exposes the one constant in our lives—the love of God.

If only Leah had been able to embrace God's love for her as she strove to gain the affection of a husband who did not love her! But the flood of rejection Leah felt every time Jacob's eyes followed her sister Rachel—his second wife—across the room caught her up in a tidal wave of manipulation. The more Leah tried to win Jacob's heart, the farther away he seemed. Each child she bore was a plea for his attention instead of a celebration of the gift God had given to fill the gap in her life. Each plea went unanswered, leaving her in despair until she finally came to the place of quiet acceptance. Reaching past the provocation to give in to resignation, Leah uttered the wisest words she could ever say and left the door open for God to usher her into a new place of peace:

"This time I will praise the LORD" (Genesis 29:35).

Oh, the stories I could tell! Tales of heartache and woe. The things that people in and out of the Bible have been through prove my point that one can survive the hatred of those who should love you. The rejection of the one you chose to give your heart and your all to. The death of a loved one—either physically, emotionally, or mentally due to drugs, a dangerous lifestyle, or the natural course of life. The violation of your most intimate parts by a stranger or, even worse, by someone you know. But this book is not about them. It is about you and what you are presently going through. You are not alone. I want to help, if that's alright with you. But you must promise me one thing. You must promise not to skip one exercise, no matter how painful it may be. Remember that pain can be a powerful teacher. It exposes the secrets that harbor defeat.

So we are going to clean house. We are going to take it slow. Layer upon layer, line upon line, until we get through this thing together. Are you ready? Now grab a pen or a pencil and take a deep breath. This is the beginning of your journey to a better you, so let's record today's date: _____

Now let's start from the beginning. Tell me what happened.

Do you remember the moment it happened? Where were you? What was going on around you? What changed?

What was your first reaction? How did you feel? (These are two different questions. I want you to separate your actions from your feelings.)

What was the response?

Was this the response that you expected?

What response did you hope for?

What was your reaction to the response? In hindsight, was your first reaction appropriate? Do you feel the response was driven by your reaction? What could you have done differently? Would it really have made a difference?

Who did you blame at the conclusion of the matter? Why?

What conclusion about yourself have you come to because of this situation? About the other person involved?

What vow have you uttered concerning this situation?

Now hold that thought, and let's move on.

In all your ways acknowledge him, and he will make your paths straight. Do not be wise in your own eyes; fear the LORD and shun evil. This will bring health to your body and nourishment to your bones.

Proverbs 3:6-8

2

Adam, Where Art Thou?

So where are you now? Someone clever once wrote that denial is not a river in Egypt. Well, you could have fooled me! It seems as if I have washed myself off in that river several times. I've stayed wet for awhile, too—that is, until the Son dried me off and brought me back to reality. Back to reality. How can three little words sound so harsh? Reality is not a popular tourist attraction. Few like going there. Perhaps that's because reality asks too many questions and brings to the surface too many emotions that one would rather not deal with.

It's so much easier to just give a glossy, "I'm fine," in response to the question "How are you?" I have a male friend who always says, "I know you're fine [attractive], but I asked you how you were feeling, not what you look like." And so it is with God. He doesn't ask us, "How are you?" He already knows that. But He does ask us, *"Where* are you?" Hmmm, now *that's* another question. Of course *He* knows where we are, but do *we* know where we are? And do we want to *admit* where we are? That is the greater challenge! Most of the time the answer to that is, "Absolutely not." To acknowledge where we are means we have to deal with how we got there. Or we might actually have to take God's suggestions on how to get out of where we presently stand. And that might just be too much work. Eeugh! God forbid we have to do the work! I'm telling you, this love business is not all it's cracked up to be. But unfortunately, until we admit where we are, we can get no farther.

Perhaps you've already figured out that the scarier side of the coin is to admit where you are and thus totally expose your needs and your vulnerabilities. And that, my friend, is just straight-out pride. How dare you take your vulnerabilities so personally? After all, everyone has the same needs—to be loved, nourished, and understood. Those needs are actually quite healthy. But in the face of pain, they become emotions that leave us feeling naked and ashamed. Like Adam.

And, like Adam, we will find that our failure to be honest with ourselves and with God leaves us vacillating between three options—fear, shame, or blame—none of which helped Adam to make any headway with God on the fateful evening after the apple (or whatever fruit it was that he and Eve ate that day) incident. I often wonder what would have happened if Adam had just told God the real deal instead of hedging on the subject. Yet I believe Adam had no idea of the depth of God's compassion, nor how passionately God wanted to preserve the relationship between Himself and mankind. So Adam skirted the issue. He was ashamed because he knew that he had failed God and failed his new bride by not being the man he was supposed to be. He knew he had not followed God's orders. He had to get the spotlight off of himself as quickly as possible, so he blamed Eve for seducing him into disobedience. And then he blamed *God* for giving him the woman to seduce him! After all, everything had been cool between them before *she* showed up...well, gee! But this is what we all do when we are not ready to deal with ourselves, when we stand in fear of what God will have to say about us if we are honest. This is why children lie to their parents—fear of punishment. Yet that is a perverted concept of God's heart toward us. He is much nicer than we perceive Him to be. He doesn't add insult to injury by berating us. He instead seeks to find a solution to our predicament.

> "Come now, let us **reason together**," says the LORD. 'Though your sins are like scarlet, they shall be as white as snow; though they are red as crimson, they shall be like wool" (Isaiah 1:18, emphasis mine).

God says, "Come on, we can sort this out if you'll just be honest with yourself and be honest with Me. I can fix it for you." But there is the rub. We are ashamed of our seeming failures and mistakes. We don't like admitting weaknesses. Yet none of this means anything to God. He anticipated our falls long before we arrived on planet Earth and already had made compensation for them through His Son Jesus. He expected you to do exactly what you did, to go through exactly what you have gone through. And now He waits for you to come to Him, ready and willing to apply the solution He has already prepared for your situation.

Tell Me Where It Hurts

Before we can expect even the world's greatest physician to cure our ills, we must be able to say what is wrong, to point to where it hurts. We must be able to describe the pain and explain when and how we first noticed it. Does it persist or does it come and go? Did you do something that could possibly have set it off? What is your diet like? What type of work do you do? Are you under stress? Do you exercise? All kinds of information is gathered in order to reach the correct diagnosis. Once the doctor makes the diagnosis, the right medication or treatment can be prescribed. Sometimes a change of lifestyle might be suggested. All of these things are decided upon in the interest of curing your ills.

When it comes to our hearts, we must be willing to be honest or we will become stuck. We will not be able to move forward if we are not able to locate the state of our hearts. No one can help us, and we can't help ourselves. But God can help us. He is able to interpret the hidden mysteries of our hearts for us. He knows us better than we know ourselves. This the Psalmist knew well.

> "Search **me**, O **God**, and know my heart; test **me** and know my anxious thoughts" (Psalm 139:23, emphasis mine).

In the book of Daniel, poor King Nebuchadnezzar had a dream that troubled him deeply. When he called for the sorcerers and the wise men to come and interpret the dream for him, the king asked them to first tell him what he had dreamt. Of course they could not. Even under the threat of death, they could not.

Sometimes the pain we feel goes so deep that we are unable to vocalize it, unable to pinpoint it. Not quite sure ourselves of what is truly wrong, we remain silent prisoners of our pain and frustration. But as Daniel was quick to tell the king, we serve a God who is the revealer of secrets. He is able to pinpoint the problem and show us exactly what is going on with us. He is able to point us toward victory if we are willing to submit to His probing and if we are ready to receive the truth. Remember, He won't cut corners. He is more concerned about our healing than about our surface sensitivities.

> "He reveals deep and hidden things; he knows what lies in darkness, and light dwells with him" (Daniel 2:22).

> "The lamp of the LORD **searches** the spirit of a man; it **searches** out his inmost being" (Proverbs 20:27, emphasis mine).

> "And he who **searches** our hearts knows the mind of the Spirit, because the Spirit intercedes for the saints in accordance with God's will" (Romans 8:27, emphasis mine).

Having trouble locating exactly how you feel? Ask Him to shed His light on the subject. This is crucial to the healing process. You must be able to honestly assess where you are.

If you were to call any mass transit authority in any city and ask for directions to a desired location, the information agent would ask, "Where are you now?" Based on your location, the agent could then map out the most effective route in order to get you where you want to go.

Want to get to the place of healing? Where are you now? Some will have a longer trip to make than others.

Tell It Like It Is

Be honest about your feelings. All of them—the good, the bad, and the ugly. God already knows how you feel anyway, so you might as well let it all hang out. He wants you to say it out loud so that you can hear it. So that you can know what you stand in need of. So that you will not move until your healing is complete. Sometimes we are ready to move before God is finished with us. When Jesus healed the blind man, it was clear that even though the man had regained his sight, his perspective was still a little off.

> "He took the blind man by the hand and led him outside the village. When he had spit on the man's eyes and put his hands on him, Jesus asked, 'Do you see anything?' He looked up and said, 'I see people; they look like trees walking around.' Once more Jesus put his hands on the man's eyes. Then his eyes were opened, his sight was restored, and he saw everything clearly" (Mark 8:23-25).

Several things become clear here. In order for this man to be healed, he had to be removed from his normal environment. All the familiar haunts and friends. All the things that supported and played into his handicap. All the things that assisted him in remaining as he was because they made compensations for his helplessness. Jesus touched him and he was healed, or so we thought until Jesus asked him a question. This is when we learn that though the man had regained his sight, his perspective was perverted. He required another touch from Jesus to make things right.

Sometimes even though God gets us over the first shock of what we have gone through, we can end up with a twisted view of our situation. We see our problems as being greater than they really are. We draw unhealthy conclusions about them and make protective vows that place us in invisible bondage. We set ourselves up for further injury because we do not see things clearly. We do not complete the healing process. We are still not free. It's like not finishing a prescription because you felt better after you took the first few pills. If you don't complete the entire course of medication, you stand a great chance of suffering a relapse.

Somewhere along the way most of us bought into a lie. The lie is simply this—that transparency and honesty are negative signs of weakness. To admit that you are hurt, afraid, disappointed, or grieving over a loss is to admit that you are not strong enough to handle your life. This is true, accept it. None of us were created to handle life on our own. We were all born with a built-in dependence upon God. So celebrate your lack of autonomy; it means that you are spiritually in tune. Don't hide from what you feel. Pain is a wonderful indicator that you are indeed human and that you possess an incredible capacity for joy. Your level of joy can only be as great as your ability to register pain. You can't recognize one without experiencing the other. Yet we see "men as trees"—their opinions mean more than they should. So, to save face, we suffer in silence.

Or perhaps it's not the opinions of others that you're so worried about. Perhaps it is the fear of what God would have to say if you were totally honest. The beautiful thing about God is that even when He speaks the truth, He speaks it with compassion—unlike some folks in our lives. I love the story of the encounter Jesus had with the Samaritan woman at the well.

> "'I have no husband,' she replied. Jesus said to her, 'You are right when you say you have no husband. The fact is, you have had five husbands, and the man you now have is not your husband. What you have just said is quite true'" (John 4:17,18).

Can you imagine? Someone calling you an adulterer to your face? Yet something in the way He said it, something in the way He looked at her, let her know He did not hold her in scorn but rather in merciful regard. He didn't get religious on her; He stayed as real as her need for love was. He offered her a way out because she was willing to be honest with Him, no matter how embarrassing that might prove to be. Jesus offers us the same opportunity, to face the truth in order to locate the real need. Only then can His touch be applied. We must be willing to become naked and unashamed in order to experience God's loving cleansing and covering of our exposed wounds.

Perhaps it hurts too much to look at those wounds, to see yourself in such a scarred condition. Is the serpent sitting on your shoulder belittling you, blaming you for what has occurred? Are you questioning your own judgment? Your own desirability? Your identity? Your sexuality? Your ability to find and maintain true happiness?

Or have you set up a memorial to your suffering? Are you wearing your pain as a badge of honor to impress others of your endurance or to fortify yourself against further onslaughts? If you are, you have opened the door to deception, which will rob you of your healing. Not feeling anything is still feeling something. Numbness is an unde-sirable sensation. It lets us know that something is wrong. Your system is in trouble. Your nerve endings are dead, not functioning. They can no longer discern danger. Reflexes are shut down, unable to rescue you by instinct. They have been silenced by your inability to feel. Numbness exposes you to that which threatens your soundness. So pinch yourself. Scream "ouch!" by all means. Feel what you feel, and say so. Light a fire. Wave a red flag. Flail your arms. Use whatever you must use and do whatever you must do to draw attention to where you are. Be willing to be rescued. Don't stay on the uncharted island of self-imposed misery.

Dare to be honest. Dare to be naked and transparent. Speak your mind. Interpret your heart. Whisper it. Speak it. Shout it. Write it. Whichever way you need to express it, do it. Whatever way, just pick a day to get real. Get funky, lowdown, honest, whether the truth hurts or not. Grit your teeth and pull out the bullet so that you can get on with the business of healing. No one said it would be easy, but it is necessary. So are you ready? It's time to end this drama. Alright, I'm ready if you are!

Where are you emotionally? Intellectually? Physically? Spiritually?

Where does it hurt? Can you explain the sensation? What sets it off?

How does this affect your health? Your day? Your capacity to function?

How does it affect your response to others around you?

How would you respond if someone approached you romantically right now?

Has your ability to trust others been affected? Why?

Are you fearful about the future? What specific areas?

What concerns you the most?

Are you ashamed of what happened? If yes, why?

Are you able to locate God's love for you in the midst of this?

What do you think God thinks of your situation? Do you care what He thinks?

Why do you think He allowed this to happen? Do you see His wisdom in it?

What are you questioning about God? About yourself?

Ahhh...now we're getting somewhere!

*I*n your anger **do not sin**; when you are on your beds, search your hearts and be silent.

Psalm 4:4, emphasis mine

3

Hell Hath No Fury . . .

The women sitting in the movie theater with me watched in fascinated horror as a scorned wife set her ex-husband's car on fire along with his clothing inside of it. Collectively, a sigh of satisfaction was released. We could all relate. Of course, that unfeeling man who had decided to ditch a twenty-year marriage for a younger model of a wife deserved worse than what he had gotten. One had to stifle the urge to shout out loud an indignant, "Off with his head!" No, none of us were amused by the pain of our sister on the screen. She had worked to put her man through school, and now that he was a successful businessman, this was her reward? To be told that she wasn't wanted anymore and that she should just accept it? I don't *think* so! Yes, her pain became my pain. And to borrow the phrase of a famous comedian, "I'm not saying that I would have burned up the man's Mercedes and designer clothing...but I can understand it."

We don't talk about anger a lot because it's just not...well...*Christian* to be angry. Or so goes the perception. Yet it is a normal, natural emotion to have—Christian or not—when we feel we have been wronged. It has nothing to do with faith. It is simply an issue of humanity. It's true that when someone hurts you, the desire to hurt that person is intense. After all, how dare he go on skipping over the rainbow, enjoying life and smelling the daisies, while you writhe in agony from the wound he inflicted on your heart? It's just not fair! No matter how calmly you face heartbreak and the violation of your emotions, eventually anger will rear its ugly head. It has to. It is the normal response to disappointment. Expectations are interesting things. Expectations believe they have the right to be fulfilled. Anger is the response to what we see as violated rights. It is my right to be loved, respected, and protected. Is it really? By whom? We will revisit this issue in a little while.

Anger can take you on a roller coaster ride that is difficult to get off of. Anger is deceptive. It gets you focused on things that will not solve your suffering. The frustration of dwelling on the fact that the other party has not paid dearly enough for what you are going through takes you further and further away from your healing. But let's deal with the source of your anger. Who are you really angry with?

The Fickle Finger of Fury

The question of who you are angry with must be answered, either now or later. Running from the truth only seems to intensify what we feel. Anger can be like quicksand. The more we fight against it, the deeper we get sucked in. But releasing yourself in the midst of it actually allows you to float to the top. So release the truth about where you are. You are angry at yourself because there is a part of you that feels you should have been more responsible for your heart. The spirit of condemnation sets in, accusing you of being a fool. Of being weak. Not sharp enough to see what was coming. How could you have let this happen? You cannot really control the actions of another, yet absorbing the blame becomes the root of the issue. Did you put yourself in position for a good hurting, or were you an innocent victim? While the jury is still out on that question, self-reproach runs rampant, causing you to despise yourself. This makes you angrier because someone who was supposed to love you has put you in the position of questioning your own worth.

Of course you are angry with the person who has put you in this state. How dare he treat you this way? You did nothing to deserve what you've gotten from him. How would he feel if the same thing was done to him? Would he be able to handle it? Would the perpetrator of his pain get off as easily? To watch him go unpunished only heightens your feelings of helplessness. Powerlessness is not an emotion that we like. It only aggravates our tempers all the more! Am I telling the truth or what?

And then, finally, there's God completing the three-pronged fork of anger. Yes, admit it. You are angry at Him, too. How could He have allowed this to happen? Isn't He supposed to take better care of your heart? Your body? Your emotions? Everything concerning you? Where was He when the upset occurred? Where is He now? Why doesn't He deal with the other person? If He won't give

His protection, then can't He at least offer justice? Yet He seems strangely silent in the midst of your distress. This only adds fuel to the flames of your exasperation. Am I hitting all the right buttons here?

Right about now we need to stop because if we continue to careen down this path, we will hurt ourselves. Anger does not afford us the luxury of thinking clearly. We are open to certain self-destruction if our emotions are allowed to run unchecked. So press the pause button until we can get to the end of this tape.

> "Like a **city** that is broken into and without **walls** is a man who has no control over his spirit" (Proverbs 25:28 NASB, emphasis mine).

We do not want to go to that city. Defenseless and in ruins is not a look that is becoming to any child of God. Yet anger causes us to pay more attention to what the flesh is screaming than what the spirit is whispering, and we find ourselves out of control, zooming down the path of bad behavior and irrational conversations, reaping embarrassing results, which then spur us on to even greater heights of frustration and foolish attempts at recovery and vengeance. No comfort can be found on this course; it's a train wreck waiting to happen. And guess who will be hurt all the more at the end of the day?

Burn, Baby, Burn

The story of Samson, found in Chapter 14 in the book of Judges, gives us a vivid look at the cycle of pain that can occur when we react in anger to love gone wrong. The story goes like this: Samson meets a woman, falls in love, and marries her. At the wedding feast, he devises a riddle for the wedding guests. If they don't solve the riddle, they will owe him thirty suits, so to speak. Well, the guests are none too happy about this massive expense they are about to incur upon themselves, so they threaten Samson's bride in order to secure the answer from her. So the new bride wheedles her husband Samson until she gets the answer, which she promptly tells to the guests. Not a very bright girl!

Needless to say, Samson was not a happy camper when he found out he had been betrayed by his new bride and now owed his guests thirty suits. So he went on a vengeful killing spree, murdering thirty men in order to deliver the thirty suits that he owed his visitors. On that note, he went to his father's house to cool down and regain his composure. By the time he was ready to kiss and make up with his wife, he discovered that, in his absence, his bride had been given to the best man! Well, you better believe that didn't help Samson get a grip on himself one bit.

> "Samson said to them, 'This time I have a right to get even with the Philistines; I will really harm them.' So he went out and caught three hundred foxes and tied them tail to tail in pairs. He then fastened a torch to every pair of tails, lit the torches and let the foxes loose in the standing grain of the Philistines. He burned up the shocks and standing grain, together with the vineyards and olive groves" (Judges 15:3-5).

Now think about this. Gathering three hundred live foxes. Tying their tails together—with torches, no less! Lighting, let's see, one, two...one hundred and fifty torches on the tails of those three hundred live foxes. This took some time, deliberation, focus, and immense physical effort. That type of cold, calculating anger is dangerous. It is deceptive because it looks so collected on the outside, but inside what builds into a raging inferno flips over to autopilot. It doesn't allow the heart to feel anything until it has done its deed. It stops at nothing to hurt others as it seeks to assuage its own pain. It feels justified in its actions and puts others at risk. This is the course of anger left unchecked. It grows to unreasonable proportions. You will see the most sophisticated sister, the nicest man, turn into a bad imitation of a creature straight out of a horror movie. Out of control. Merciless. Wreaking havoc. Hideous.

Yet God says, "Be angry and sin not." That almost seems to be a contradictory statement. How can you be angry and not sin? It's possible only if you know where to place your anger.

> "Do not take revenge, my friends, but leave room for God's wrath, for it is written: 'It is **mine** to avenge; I will repay,' says the Lord" (Romans 12:19, emphasis mine).

> "It is **mine** to avenge; I will repay. In due time their foot will slip; their day of disaster is near and their doom rushes upon them" (Deuteronomy 32:35, emphasis mine).

There. Doesn't that make you feel better? So where do we put our anger? We place it in the hands of the One who knows how to hold the reins. God understands. He Himself gets angry, so He won't fault you on that. What He *will* hold you accountable for is how you express your anger. By seeking to punish your offender, you have rendered judgment. This is not your job. God is the One who decides which punishment goes with each wrong deed done. He is the only One who can do this fairly because

He is the only One who has all the details—the whys, the hows, and the wherefores. Therefore, leave it in His hands.

Caught in a Fix

Samson got in trouble because he took matters into his own hands. The more he pursued his own retribution, the deeper the situation got. Others were endangered. Others—including his ex-wife and father-in-law—were *killed* because of his escapades! Anger is like a fire out of control. It's hard to contain. The wind blows and sends it in a direction you never intended for it to go. Before you know it, things are beyond your control and you can't take back words that were said in haste or actions that were made without thinking. We miss cues. We lose discernment. Sound judgment goes out the window and we begin a cycle of mistakes that leads us into bondage. We get caught up in trying to "fix" it and find ourselves fixed instead. Then we try to fix the fix and...well, you see the vicious cycle, don't you? And all the while the quiet voice of God says, "Go ahead, be angry; just *don't sin.*"

Don't fall into unforgiveness. Don't harbor bitterness in your heart. When you do, innocent people get hurt. Besides the death of Samson's ex-wife and father-in-law because of Samson's rampage, the Israelites were threatened and had to bargain with Samson's life in order to spare themselves from the wrath of the Philistines. Now, let's break this down into an everyday scenario. We meet someone who actually would be deserving of our love, but we are unable to give or receive it after what we have suffered. Caught off-guard, this one who is innocent involuntarily bears the brunt of our past experiences. We unpack all of our old baggage in his clear view and accuse him of being guilty of the same things. Or we hide our pain and never let him get close enough to see or soothe our scars. And the cycle of pain continues because hurt people hurt other people if the flame of anger is never extinguished. It smolders deep within and flares up at inopportune moments. It destroys the soil that could be holding seed rich with new beginnings. But we can't see this through the smoke.

How do you see yourself clear? By dealing constructively and realistically with where you are. Jesus said that offenses would come, but woe to the one the offense comes through (Luke 17:1). So bank on offenses. Expect them. Life will not allow you to be disappointed on that promise. We will be hurt and offended, but the offender is already in trouble. Don't make God have to postpone dealing with him in order to deal with you. Relinquish the rights you imagine yourself having. The only right we truly have is to be possessed by Christ once we choose to become His own. All other rights have been hidden in Him. If indeed we have truly died and risen with Christ, we must be dead to the onslaughts against our hearts. If we know that offenses will come, we will no longer be rocked by them. Instead we will give them to the Father right away and not hold onto them. So stop, take a deep breath, and cut anger off at the pass. If it already has a hold on you, stop, work it out, and shake it off. How do you work with your anger? Let it expose the unsurrendered areas in your heart. Yes, we have come full circle back to the principle of violated rights. If we have truly surrendered our lives to Christ, we no longer have the right to defend ourselves. He becomes our defense. Our trust in His protection should diffuse our anger. So acknowledge the areas you've placed under your own domain, then give them back to Him.

If we are presenting our bodies as living sacrifices to God, He becomes our shield and buckler. The problem arises when we, as living sacrifices, slide off the altar and creep out from behind the protective cover that the Lord has provided for our hearts. Even when this happens, we still have the opportunity to run for cover before the sun goes down. God tells us not to carry anger over to the next day. Why? Because the more we rehearse an offense, the bigger it grows, and the more difficult it is to do away with it, the greater our bonds become.

"But don't I ever have the right to be angry?" you ask. "Isn't there ever an appropriate time to explode?" Oh, there most definitely is! Jesus was extremely angry when the merchants took over the outer court of the temple to sell their wares. The Gentiles were unable to pray in the space allocated to them because the Jews thought them unworthy to approach their God, so they set up shop. Jesus came and reminded them that it wasn't about what they thought. God had said that His temple was to be a house of prayer, not a house of merchandising. How dare they hinder someone from being able to approach God! Jesus had a righteous wrath for the rights of God. Get the difference? So, is your anger for righteous reasons or for personal reasons? If it's personal, leave your issues at the foot of the cross and allow the blood of Jesus to cover them.

Yes, you will be angry, but sin not. Someone once said that you can't stop a bird from flying over your head, but you can stop it from building a nest. Don't build a temple to house your anger. Acknowledge your anger. Tell God all about it. He looks beyond the fault and sees the need.

He sees past the walls that anger builds up to protect the heart, and He also sees the pain that you've tried to bury. Sometimes we allow anger to dominate our emotions because it feels safer and more powerful than the hurt we actually feel. It is the coward who is actually masquerading as a bully. But anger wastes our time. It delays our healing. So we need to locate it. Pinpoint it. Vocalize it. And then release it to God. Free yourself. The choice is yours.

Would the news that something unfortunate had happened to the person who hurt you make you feel better? Why?

Do you have an emotional or physical reaction (jaws get tight, blood vessels constrict, or emotions shut down) at the mention of this person's name? How much time does it take for you to regain your composure?

Fill in: I am angry at _____ because
_____
_____.

Who else are you angry at? Yourself? God? Why?

How do you feel you were wronged? How do you feel
that God has failed you?

In what way do you feel God is responsible for you?
Which Scriptures confirm what you believe?

What part have you been given in being responsible for
yourself? Have you exercised responsibility, cooperated
with the Holy Spirit, or taken God's protection for granted?

Do you feel victimized by the person who hurt you? In what way?

What would this person have to do to make you feel better?

Is that expectation realistic?

How will you respond if your needs are not ever met by this person?

What would you like to tell this person? Is this person in the position to receive what you have to say?

What can you do to settle this issue with yourself? With God?

What can others do to help you through this?

What frustrates you the most about this situation? About the person who hurt you? Your own ability to cope? The reactions of others?

Do you believe that things will get better with time? Why or why not?

What will change things for you?

How are you feeling at present?

What unhealthy compensations are you making to cope? Healthy compensations?

Are you willing to take things one day at a time, or are you paralyzed by the big picture of your life?

How is your relationship with God these days?

Thank you for your honesty. It is the most important step you'll ever make toward your healing.

*Y*ou turned my wailing into dancing; you removed my sackcloth and clothed me with joy, that my heart may sing to you and not be silent. O LORD my God, I will give you thanks forever.

Psalm 30:11,12

4

Under the Juniper Tree

When I recall my responses to heartbreak, I recall one heartbreak in particular that leveled my world. I found it hard to face the day. The sun was cruel for rising, in my opinion. How dare people have smiles on their faces? Didn't they know the world had come to an end? My head was heavy, my body limp. I was powerless to function. I wondered how long it would be before God would put me out of my misery. I didn't want to pretend to cope. I wanted to die. My heart echoed the sentiments of every pitiful love song I heard on the radio, and I invited the words to wash over me and confirm my misery. It was true; I would never breathe again...breathe again....There was no me without him. I wasn't inhaling or exhaling—I was merely existing and wishing I wasn't.

Depression. Not my favorite emotion. But you can count on it showing up. I think that anger and depression actually run a relay race together through our emotions. Once anger has run its course, it hands the baton over to depression. The overwhelming sadness that follows can really affect your game if you let it. It is like looking at the remains of a vast forest fire. After the raging is over, everything is black and silent. No signs of life remain. You wonder what will become of this bleak scenario.

Because anger takes so much energy, it usually bottoms out into depression. I can pretty much surmise that when Samson retreated to his father's house after his killing spree, he sat there sulking in depressed silence. Overstimulation of emotions as well as tremendous physical exertion usually preempt depression. Again, this has nothing to do with faith but everything to do with the weariness of body and soul.

We sink to the bottom of our emotions, overwhelmed by hopelessness, overcome by the flood of negative thoughts and feelings. This can knock us off-balance. We are usually surprised by these foreign guests who have taken up residence in our heart and psyche. They send us running for cover, beating a hasty retreat from that which seems to be so contrary to our faith. The voice of God sounds faint, drowned out by the voices of resignation and apathy that arrive promising deceptive relief.

> "...weeping may remain for a **night**, but rejoicing comes in the morning" (Psalm 30:5, emphasis mine).

We have this promise, but joy seems so foreign in the night of our soul. All we know is that sleep seems to be the most welcome condition. Too tired to fight for the strength to have faith, we struggle to muster a "Help me, God" before slipping into a fitful slumber.

Blowing the Fuse

Elijah, mighty man of God that he was, battled with depression. He laid down under a juniper tree and, just before he fell asleep, asked God to take his life. Let's look at the events leading up to that moment. Hmm, first Elijah repaired the altar of God that had been destroyed. Killed and prepared a sacrifice. Called down fire from heaven. Slew a hundred of Jezebel's personal prophets of Baal. Interceded for the drought in Israel to be broken and the rains to come. Outran Ahab's chariots in order to give him the news of the coming rainfall. And, last but not least, absorbed the evil threats of Jezebel, who had threatened to take his life. Small wonder Elijah got depressed! All of the above-mentioned things absorbed a lot of physical energy. When our bodies or emotions go on overload, our systems quickly move to protect themselves by shutting down. It's kind of like blowing a fuse. Everything disables or short-circuits to keep from blowing up. It is actually a safety device to force you to cool it before you hurt yourself. The body says, "Alright, girlfriend, take a chill pill before you lose it. I tell you what, I'm going to make you so sad and weary, you won't be able to do anything but sleep until you allow yourself to mend."

This is allowed for a time. But only for a time. God Himself will minister to you during this grace period. But then He will bid you to rise.

> "Then [Elijah] lay down and slept under the tree and fell asleep. All at once an angel touched him and said, 'Get up and eat.' He looked around, and

> there by his head was a cake of bread baked over hot coals, and a jar of water. He ate and drank and then lay down again. The angel of the LORD came back a second time and touched him and said, 'Get up and eat, for the journey is too much for you.' So he got up and ate and drank. Strengthened by that food, he traveled forty days and forty nights until he reached Horeb, the mount of God" (1 Kings 19:5-8).

So allow God to feed you and revive you. He knows when you've reached the end of your reserve. It is His strength that will carry you toward your healing. But in the meantime you must understand the way you take. You must not feel alone. And you must not see your depression as a sign of spiritual impotence. There are key times in our lives when depression lifts its head to stop us in our tracks. Besides the overstimulation of our senses after tremendous emotional or physical upheaval, there is the looming of a major transition in the distance. The flesh quivers against change. It strains against it and wars with the spirit. It plays a tug-of-war with your faith and the desire to move on. The cost of the journey seems overwhelming; it taxes our emotional reserves. Even Jesus struggled with this before His crucifixion.

> "Then saith [Jesus] unto them, My soul is exceeding sorrowful, even unto death: tarry ye here, and watch with me" (Matthew 26:38 KJV).

Though He knew the joy that awaited Him on the other side of the cross, the price of getting there took its toll. That price was becoming sin for us—the one thing the Father hated. Knowing that this would separate Him from the Father was almost more than He could bear. Three whole days would pass before He would be one with the Father again. Jesus would bear our sins to the cross. Die. Go to Hades. Snatch the keys of hell and death from the devil. Set the captive free. Rise from the dead. Walk the earth for several days, revealing Himself to the disciples and others, before ascending back to the Father. But those initial moments of becoming the sacrificial lamb that God could not look upon—because holiness cannot abide in the presence of sin—overwhelmed Jesus with horror.

Our flesh shrinks back in horror every time the Spirit of God asks it to die. Die to misplaced expectations. Die to our dreams and desires. Die to a relationship we longed for, counted on, built our lives around. Small wonder Jesus suffered depression in the Garden of Gethsemene. He was about to suffer the betrayal of those He loved on earth and the rejection of the One He was completely one with. A piece of Himself was being torn from Him. His very soul would be split asunder.

The Ties that Bind

Many times we fail to understand the deep significance of what happens in the spirit when we become involved with someone romantically. Depending on the depth of sharing and interaction, we can develop soul ties. If this includes being involved sexually, this becomes an even stronger bond. We become one with the other person. Whether this was a godly soul tie or not, when the relationship ends we suffer the severing of our souls. We wonder why it is so hard to recover, especially if we have come to the conclusion intellectually that our partner was not good for us. Yet this yearning to be with that person covers us like a wet blanket, smothering our joy and killing the hope of ever being able to love and be loved again.

Picture your soul as a tree in the center of your being. A person comes into your life. The two of you connect mentally, emotionally, spiritually, and physically. You become grafted into one another's spirits. Your thoughts and desires become entwined. You begin to grow into one another, much like when you join a branch into a vine. Eventually the two become one. You have now become part of one another. When the relationship is severed, when the branch is cut off from the vine or a patch of bark is stripped from the tree, the wound is evident. It is an ugly scar. Though the tree is healed and continues to grow, a mark remains, reminding us of the damage that has been done. Our spirits are affected in much the same way. Our heart is scarred. Phantom pain calls attention to the fact that someone, something, is missing from our lives. We long to extinguish the sting. So we reach for the familiar, whether the situation was good for us or not. How do you unravel yourself from someone with whom you are bound? Well, in the Bible, prayer and fasting are both encouraged for times when we need to set aside our fleshly desires and focus intently on the Lord. In Leviticus 16:29, the Israelites are commanded to "deny yourselves," which is based on a Hebrew expression that includes forsaking food as an act of self-denial.

Fasting is the denial of the flesh. It is starving yourself of whatever hinders you from hearing the Spirit and being able to receive what the Spirit of the Lord is trying to say to you—words of freedom that will bring life back into the dead places of your heart. Fasting is the key. There are lots of different ways to fast. Fasting can apply to a lot of things besides food. You might need to fast from conversations that heap more logs on the fire that is already burning out of control in your heart. You might need to fast from the person of your focus or from any thing, place, or activity that reminds you of the person or puts you in his path. You also might need to fast from anything that dredges up memories that make it hard for you to release him.

You must be willing to do whatever it takes to secure your healing. That means you must be willing to strengthen your spirit. Your spirit must become stronger than your flesh. All habits surrounding this person must be broken. This will not be easy, but that is the reality of your situation. Healing is never a simple matter. It requires some effort on your part. If you have an impacted tooth, it must be removed. If you have something that threatens the health of your body, it must be killed through medication or removed through surgery. Initially this is not a pleasant feeling, but it eventually brings the relief and health that you seek. The same applies to your heart and your spirit. This is where a personal inventory must be taken. You must select your own limits and set your own boundaries here—whatever it is for you. You must clear your decks in order to hear the word of the Lord. When Elijah lay listless under the juniper tree, God fed him just enough to strengthen him for a journey that would remove him from his situation long enough to redirect his focus.

None of us can hear God and receive liberation when our flesh is screaming in our ears. And God will not shout over the din. He comes peaceably, speaking softly, calmly, telling us profound things that strengthen us to begin again with a new attitude. Yes, He will draw near. He will even cover you for a time. But in the end He demands that we get back in the race.

"The LORD said [to Elijah], 'Go out and stand on the mountain in the presence of the LORD, for the LORD is about to pass by.' Then a great and powerful wind tore the mountains apart and shattered the rocks before the LORD, but the LORD was not in the wind. After the wind there was an earthquake, but the LORD was not in the earthquake. After the earthquake came a fire, but the LORD was not in the fire. And after the fire came a gentle whisper. When Elijah heard it, he pulled his cloak over his face and went out and stood at the mouth of the cave. Then a voice said to him, 'What are you doing here, Elijah?' He replied, 'I have been very zealous for the LORD God Almighty. The Israelites have rejected your covenant, broken down your altars, and put your prophets to death with the sword. I am the only one left, and now they are trying to kill me too.' The LORD said to him, 'Go back the way you came…'" (1 Kings 19:11-15).

God sent Elijah back the same fearful route he had come and instructed him to pick up a partner along the way—Elisha, a young man who would emerge as a powerful prophet after being under the tutelage of Elijah, this depressed man of God. God wanted Elijah to not only confront his fears by facing them, but also to know he was not alone. He would not allow him to fall prey to the lies of the enemy and stay there.

The Place of Restoration

The turbulence of our relationships can make us run for cover. It can rock the very foundation of our hearts. It can try our faith by fire, but in the midst of it all God comes speaking a soft, sure word in the center of our pain and despair. Silencing the questions, the hasty vows, all the conversations with friends, the wrenching sobs that initially drown out His voice, He deals with our feelings of isolation and hopelessness for the future by making us face our pain dead-on. He brings us not out of our pain but through it and past it, knowing that true victory is triumphing in the midst of our seeming helplessness. We are able to pass by the way of our trial again, free and whole in His strength, knowing that we are not alone. We have Him as our partner. In Him we can trust.

This can only come to pass as we sever all connections to where we have been—fast, as it were—in order to clearly see His direction. Our lifeline rests in our relationship and conversation with God. Ah, but here is the problem—when we are depressed, spent by the anger that disappointment brings, it is difficult to pray.

Hopelessness whispers, "What is the use? There is no remedy for your situation." The future stretches out before you with no high points. There is no sign of restoration in sight, only endless reminders of your loss, your pain, and your future alone. Alone! This one word echoes through the caverns of your soul, reverberates through your mind, and makes your wounded heart run for cover. The heart quivers at the thought of endless isolation. No sign of comfort. Of love. Of safety and security. Of joy and happiness. Of all the dreams you built on the foundation of your tomorrows with the one who has forsaken you. "You are hopelessly alone," the enemy sneers. Why anticipate a happy ending? Even God seems not to be listening; therefore, why try to communicate with Him or anyone else? "There is nothing you can do." Another lie, but for now it is enough to make you turn inside yourself and give in to paralysis and prayerlessness. Even the disciples struggled with this.

> "When he [Jesus] rose from prayer and went back to the disciples, he found them asleep, exhausted from sorrow. 'Why are you sleeping?' he asked them. 'Get up and pray so that you will not fall into temptation'" (Luke 22:45-46).

The temptation to remain in the place of faithlessness is great if we cut ourselves off from the only One who can solve our problems. If we do not reconnect, we will resort to taking matters into our own hands, like Samson did, and thus destroy ourselves. Remember Samson's rampage against the Philistines? Or we might decide to strike out in useless actions that solve nothing, like Peter did. Peter cut off the ear of one of the guards who came to take Jesus away. But this did not keep Jesus from going to the cross. It only got Peter into trouble. Later, one of the relatives of the man who had been attacked questioned Peter's association with the Lord, and Peter was compelled to deny Jesus in order to protect himself—something he had promised Jesus he wouldn't do. This cut him to the core, further deepening the distress he already felt over all that had transpired. Things done in haste have a way of catching up with us and causing further damage. Words cannot be taken back. Foolish moves cause greater stress on an already-fragile situation. It is an avalanche effect. Unless the word of the Lord is able to pull us back into check, we find ourselves caught up in the tide of our pain, careening down a mountain of emotions, out of control.

Like Judah, the traitorous disciple of Jesus, we will seek to end it all. To relieve ourselves of our pain. Perhaps not through physical suicide, but possibly through spiritual or emotional suicide. We might turn away from God, seeking another relationship to make us forget the former. This is merely a temporary Band-Aid, at best. If we do not allow God to deal with the wound beneath the layers we dress it in, we stand to infect our hearts and suffer a more serious malady later when the same issues or things that remind us of the past resurface in the new situation. Another failed relationship will only further complicate matters. If the avalanche effect is left unchecked, it is easy to get caught up in a recurring cycle of repeat rejection and betrayal, which will only lead us to a place of deeper despondency. This is the plan of the enemy to completely destroy us, to strip us of the one thing that can rescue and restore us—our faith.

> "**Hope deferred** makes the heart sick, but a longing fulfilled is a tree of life" (Proverbs 13:12, emphasis mine).

There is only One who is able to consistently fulfill His promises. One who will never let us down. If we give in to the disease of the heart without fighting to regain our wholeness, we lose the ability to love as God created us to love. But if we embrace what God gives us, our longing is fulfilled in Him. We are then able to become fruitful again, restored and strengthened to embrace the physical mani-festation of His love for us, should He choose to send it to us at a later time.

Until then, rest. Allow God to feed you, comfort you, cover you, and speak to you. Decide to take the journey to the mountaintop. Breathe in the clean air and let the spirit of God breathe life back into your members and hope back into your spirit. Seize the reality that you are not alone. Though the one who hurt you is not present, anticipate better tomorrows. This is not about the other person. This is about you. Be selfish for this season, for the higher call and the purposes of God. Protect the call of God upon your life and the gifts He has placed within you, one of the greatest of those being the capacity to love and feel things deeply. Yes, you are depressed, but this too shall pass if you let it.

Do you feel unusually weary? Physically? Emotionally? Spiritually? In what way?

Have you been overly stimulated physically? Emotionally? What were the events that contributed to this?

What areas of your life are suffering as a result of this? How does this affect your work? Your relationships? Your ability to function?

How are others responding to your difficulty?

Do you feel you have a network of people to support you during this time? Who are they?

Are you able to share where you are with them? If no, why not? If yes, have you been completely honest with them?

How can friends and family be a source of support for you? What do you need from them?

Are friends and family capable of providing what you need at this time?

Do you feel isolated? If yes, why?

What would it take to make you see that you are not alone?

Do you feel hopeless? If yes, why?

What were your hopes before? Which of your dreams have been lost because of this occurrence?

Were your expectations toward the person who hurt you misplaced? What about your expectations toward yourself? Toward God? In what way?

Were your efforts misdirected? In what way? What was your focus? What should it have been?

What can you do to get back on course?

What would it take to renew your joy? Is this a realistic request? Is it a healthy request?

What new hopes can you have? Who will be the source of fulfilling these?

Remember, this too shall pass, so hold on and move forward.

*D*o not be anxious about anything, but in everything, by prayer and petition, with thanksgiving, present your requests to God. And the peace of God, which transcends all understanding, will guard your hearts and your minds in Christ Jesus.

Philippians 4:6,7

5

Coming Clean

hat is it about prayer, especially when we are hurting? It often seems like we'd rather talk to anyone but God. Have you ever found yourself in the place where you tried to reach every friend you have in order to pour out your heart and get a few words of comfort? To your chagrin, every number renders the same results—no one home. And you know deep inside of yourself that God is waiting...patiently waiting for you to come to Him. But whether out of anger, shame, or the desire for a more immediate and audible answer, you fight against running to the arms of the only One who holds the answer to your situation.

> "'**Come** now, let us **reason together**,' says the LORD. 'Though your sins are like scarlet, they shall

be as white as snow; though they are red as crimson, they shall be like wool'" (Isaiah 1:18, emphasis mine).

"If any of you lacks **wisdom**, he should **ask God**, who gives generously to all without finding fault, and it will be given to him" (James 1:5, emphasis mine).

Certainly God is approachable. Whether we are the victimized or the guilty, He is open to communication. He wants to work things out. Besides being too sorrowful to speak, what other things keep us from talking to the ultimate Comforter? Hmm, let's see…could it be the adversary, the enemy of your soul? He comes accusing God of not caring, of not being able to relate to your pain, of being condescending and judgmental, of being someone who won't take your part. Somehow he twists the scenario and makes the painful events all your fault. He piles condemnation on top of your fresh anguish. If what he says is true, you can't possibly go to God. It would be more than you could bear to have Him agree that you did something so unlovely that it rendered you unloveable. But we delay hearing words to the contrary because we shut down and turn away from Him.

If you are of the persuasion that prayer is indeed a two-way conversation—one where you talk to God and He answers—you tend to be a bit more careful about entering into discussion with Him. After all, when He speaks, not a word is wasted—and it usually requires action on our part. Whether it be letting go, taking the bull by the horns, or moving on, God will call for something from us. If we are too tired to do the work, then we cannot pursue a solution. If we are faithless, we simply resign and don't even bother to inquire if any hope remains. If we don't think that we will like His answer, we avoid the issue. If we decide that He will tell us something we don't want to hear, we cut Him off at the pass.

Whatever the emotion, the bottom line is the same—prayerlessness on your part, which will only lead to certain paralysis and bondage. And on that note, the enemy of your soul delights in your defeat. To cut you off from every relationship of significance—especially your relationship with God—is his primary mission. Yes, estrangement from God is of paramount importance in his plan to destroy you. He wants to keep you from the One who has the ability to heal and free you, to keep you from receiving the words that could break the shackles from your spirit. All of this fits perfectly into the plan of the one who comes to steal our joy and confidence, kill our faith, and destroy our souls. He knows that the truth will make us free. Therefore, he will help us avoid the One who will tell us the truth at all costs. If we don't talk to God, we will never hear the truth. And God, being the gentleman that He is, will not push Himself upon us. He waits…and waits…and waits until we are ready to come to Him. He will not speak until He knows that we are ready to hear what He has to say. He will not waste His breath because there is life in it, and life cannot be treated carelessly.

The Silent Treatment

I must admit that I am a lot like Jonah, who ran from the presence of God and wound up in the belly of the whale. Jonah held a little standoff with God. I kind of get this picture of him sitting in that smelly carcass just *extremely* aggravated at God, refusing to say a word. Knowing he had gotten himself into this pickle, Jonah was just too, too, *too* upset to deal with it, and so he simply sat there with his arms folded, jaw set, determined to hold his breath for ransom. As if that would make God see things his way! Well, things just don't work that way, Jonah soon found out.

> "But the LORD provided a great fish to swallow Jonah, and Jonah was inside the fish three days and three nights. From inside the fish Jonah prayed to the LORD his God. He said: 'In my distress I called to the LORD, and he answered me. From the depths of the grave I called for help, and you listened to my cry....When my life was ebbing away, I remembered you, LORD, and my prayer rose to you, to your holy temple. Those who cling to worthless idols forfeit the grace that could be theirs. But I, with a song of thanksgiving, will sacrifice to you. What I have vowed I will make good. Salvation comes from the LORD.' And the LORD commanded the fish, and it vomited Jonah onto dry land" (Jonah 1:17; 2:1,2,7-10).

Truly, when we turn from the outstretched arms of a helpful God, the issues of life and our personal dilemmas swallow us up. And God allows them to. The story goes that Jonah was in his underwater prison for three days. Depending on the translation, we are told that *then* Jonah prayed. After three days! Now, I don't know about you, but I think I would have been calling on the name of Jesus before I even hit the water. Jonah, though, was a stubborn ole thang. And in this case, the only thing a hard head got him was a soggy tush. But on the third day, Master J came to his senses, realized something significant, and began to rap. Those who cling to worthless idols forfeit the grace that could be theirs. They don't have open hands to receive any blessings.

What was Jonah holding onto? His own agenda. His own idea of how God should work things out. He had definite ideas about how God should treat his enemies and somehow he had this gut feeling (no pun intended) that God was going to be a whole lot nicer to them than he wanted Him to be. Well, Jonah thought, God would have to choose between him and those nasty Ninevites. He would just stand his ground. He finally realized that he wasn't getting anywhere, only more and more water-logged. As he came to the end of himself, Jonah realized he could no longer ignore the lifeline that God was willing to throw to him. As he called out to God, the Lord delivered him onto dry land. Without prayer we have nothing to stand on, nowhere to turn to find the relief we seek.

Jonah not only finally broke through the silence with God, he also went a step farther. He made a sacrifice of praise. *Praise?! Oh, don't even go there! I'm not ready for that!* you say. I hear you, but we must. Notice it was called a sacrifice. Jonah didn't feel like praising God either. He was not a happy camper. As far as he was concerned, there was nothing to praise God about. Yet he yielded to the knowledge of God's sovereignty and the fact that He knew best. Once this was established, God could free him.

Giving Up the Praise

Something happens when we praise God. First we are forced to acknowledge His goodness and all the wonderful things He has done for us in the past. As we begin the litany, it puts us in remembrance of what He is able to do in our lives. If He was able to do *that* then, why can't He fix *this* now? Yes, one look at our spiritual trophy case reminds us that God is able. We have suffered and been revived before. The more we rehearse His goodness, the happier we get. This is why we must fight to get to the place of worship and praise. This accomplishes things that all your other efforts won't. It breaks up the spiritual atmosphere and puts darkness to flight. It opens the door for light to come in and illuminate not only your understanding but also your circumstance. It causes God to come closer, and trouble cannot remain in God's presence. David, the king of Israel, understood this concept well. After the death of a son born out of an adulterous affair and being betrayed by his own son, he didn't feel like praising and worshipping, but he spoke to himself until he did.

> "Praise the LORD, O my soul; all my inmost being, praise his holy name. Praise the LORD, O my soul, and forget not all his benefits—who forgives all your sins and heals all your diseases, who redeems your life from the pit and crowns you with love and compassion, who satisfies your desires with good things so that your youth is renewed like the eagle's. The LORD works righteousness and justice for all the oppressed" (Psalm 103:1-6).

Yeah, David had to talk to himself and remind himself why he should praise the Lord. He ran down an entire litany and by the time he was finished, I get a picture of him beginning to dance, he was feeling so good. The shackles fell off and wholeness and joy began to flood his being. The chains around his heart disintegrated and he was captivated only by a spirit of liberation. His enemies?

They were still there but they no longer mattered. His troubles? The solutions hadn't yet manifested themselves, but that wasn't his focus. His knowledge of the outcome? He didn't really know. All he knew was that God was still on the throne and whatever He chose to do was just, fair, and the best thing for all concerned. Victory was guaranteed. This he could be sure of because of past experiences. This gave him a reason to celebrate though nothing in his world looked different to the human eye. He was sure that things looked vastly different from heaven's perspective. All he had to do was wait for it to materialize in the natural realm. He knew he served a God who was on His side, a God who loved him passionately, an all-powerful God who did all things well. Secure in his knowledge of these three things, David could believe for the victory. He would praise Him, await His instruction, and yield to it, knowing that God's word always paves the way to victory.

Processing the Process

The great question is this: Are we ready to hear God's solution? His answers are not usually what we have in mind when we first approach Him. Hearing the truth requires action on our part—action that we find hard to savor. Regardless of what happened or who hurt or offended us, God requires us to deal with ourselves first. When we come to God pointing to the problem, He calmly says, "What about *you*?" He deals with problems from the inside out. It is not the *problem* that is a problem; it is our own ability to hinder our wholeness. We usually prefer to avoid the process that is required for our healing.

We don't want to get our hands dirty. We don't want to do the work it takes to get to the other side of our pain.

The story goes that Naaman was a mighty warrior. But even the strongest can be afflicted with issues beyond their control. Naaman was told that there was a mighty man of God who had the answer for the healing he needed.

> "So Naaman went with his horses and chariots and stopped at the door of Elisha's house. Elisha sent a messenger to say to him, 'Go, wash yourself seven times in the Jordan, and your flesh will be restored and you will be cleansed.' But Naaman went away angry and said, 'I thought that he would surely come out to me and stand and call on the name of the LORD his God, wave his hand over the spot and cure me of my leprosy. Are not Abana and Pharpar, the rivers of Damascus, better than any of the waters of Israel? Couldn't I wash in them and be cleansed?' So he turned and went off in a rage. Naaman's servants went to him and said, 'My father, if the prophet had told you to do some great thing, would you not have done it? How much more, then, when he tells you, "Wash and be cleansed"?' So he went down and dipped himself in the Jordan seven times, as the man of God had told him, and his flesh was restored and became clean like that of a young boy" (2 Kings 5:9-14).

We, too, would like God to wave a magic wand over our hearts and make us whole in a snap. We also sometimes wonder why He can't work the pain out of our system in an easier or prettier way. Why must we get down to the nitty-gritty by actually dealing with ourselves and our emotions? Why must we deal with getting past anger, putting into practice forgiveness (which we'll get to later!), and getting over ourselves and our perception of our rights? Yet He says to us, "Wash and be cleansed." *Cleansed of what, Lord?* Cleansed of all attitudes, thoughts, words, and actions that separate us from Him, that separate us from the source of our healing—the things that we naturally give in to when we are in pain, or have been deeply offended. Though we might be justified and in the right, we should still desire to cleanse ourselves of any residue of transgression that might stain us. We need to purpose to attain a new level of maturity in the midst of our search for restoration. We must realize that growth and healing cost something. We cannot remain unwilling to get real with God about our situation, to refuse to be completely vulnerable to His word and His touch.

Neither can we be hindered by what we feel God should do to our offender. Like Jonah who could not get past the idea that God should punish the Ninevites, we will find ourselves separated from God because of this attitude. Jonah became consumed with judgmental thoughts instead of trusting God to deal with their hearts and turn them from their wicked ways. Meanwhile, God knew that the Ninevites were not beyond reach, though Jonah wanted them to be. Jonah put his own relationship with God in jeopardy because he got fixated on longing for the demise of others. His vengeful feelings got in the way of his own ability to move forward in life and his own ability to converse with God.

The Right Prescription

It is important to deal with the reality that the only soul we can control is our own. The fate of all others will be decided by God based on their actions, which He fairly takes into account. His motivation for dealing with your offender will not be the same as yours. God is motivated by the need for salvation, not vengeance. In His determination to bring others to repentance, He allows them to reap what they sow. Eventually the fish of life that swallows us whole will cause us to look up to Him, if we are wise. If we are not, we will sink in the midst of our own bad choices. Keeping the line open between ourselves and God is the only way to be able to make sound life decisions.

But even in these momentary lapses, God understands and waits patiently for you to come to Him. He feels your pain and longs to talk to you about it. He wants to apply His healing balm to your wounded heart and to cover your scars with His loving hands. He has the perfect prescription to heal you, but you must be willing to receive it and take the full course. You must be willing to yield to the ministrations of the Chief Physician. To resist His touch, to ignore His prescription, is to prolong your pain.

"Oh, what peace we often forfeit; oh, what needless pain we bear. All because we do not carry everything to God in prayer."

When was the last time you had a heart-to-heart talk with God?

What has hindered you from reaching out to Him?

If you have been talking to Him, have you been completely honest with Him about your feelings?

What are you afraid of seeing about your situation if you become completely transparent? About yourself? About the other person? About your actions and responses to what has happened?

What are you clinging to in this relationship?

What do you feel your rights are in this situation? Why are these things dear to you? What would it really cost you to let go?

Why is letting go so hard? What do you think it will cost you? Is that true? Can that be viewed as a positive?

Are you willing to surrender what you think should happen in your situation? What is your greatest fear connected to this thought?

What can you do to help yourself let go? What boundaries can you set? What things should you avoid?

What are your areas of weakness concerning the other person? What do you need from God to get stronger? How can you cooperate with Him?

What has kept you from cooperating so far?

What do you think will happen if you do things God's way? What will happen if you don't?

Do you trust God enough to turn this over to Him?

Get a cup of tea, and invite the Lord to join you. Pour out your feelings as you would to an old friend. After all, He is the friend who sticks closer than a brother. Don't be afraid to be honest with Him about every aspect of your thoughts and emotions. Now sip your tea and wait for Him to answer. He will.

*C*ast all your anxiety on him because he **cares** for you.

1 Peter 5:7, emphasis mine

6

Balloons
in the Wind

very time I recall my girl Jennifer Holliday belting out the words, "And I'm telling you I'm not going…" in the Broadway play *Dreamgirls*, I have to shake my head. Her man wanted out of the relationship, and she wasn't ready for that at all. She was willing to hold on until she could hold on no longer. I can relate to that, but it's not a very healthy place to be in. As a matter of fact, it usually leaves us feeling worse than if we had just let go and gotten the pain over with. But now we pile shame on top of the pain by forcing the other person to give us a forceful boot, as opposed to carefully extricating themselves from our hearts. Some of us stand, nursing the pain, by having a relationship with the other person all by ourselves. Holding on to that person in our minds and hearts, clinging to the last good sentiments that we can remember and romanticizing even the bad parts of the relationship. That, of course, only takes our pain to a deeper level.

Almost every song we hear about broken relationships cries a woeful tale of "there is no me without you." I can't breathe again, inhale, exhale, survive, or make it through another day. We've all indulged ourselves in the misery these songs share, comforted in a dysfunctional kind of way that someone else can relate to where we are. I can relate, too, but I still say, *snap out of it!*

The truth of the matter is, there *is* you whether someone is with you or not. And admit it, you're breathing in and out right now as you are reading this. You will get up again tomorrow whether you like it or not. How you plan to deal with the day is completely up to you. However, your ability to possess your day will be hindered if you are still holding on to something else—namely, dead weight. It's true, the severing of a relationship is much like experiencing the death of a loved one. The only difference is, with death we are forced to let go of the other person. We have no other choice. But when the person whom we love is still walking around in the flesh, it's like a carrot being waved under our noses, just out of our reach. It hurts. It hurts to not be able to reach out and take hold of what we want so badly. So, what do we do? The answer is simple: Let go.

Hold out your hands and allow the Holy Spirit to lovingly pry your unwilling fingers off of the other person. The secret to moving on is release. Whether your shattered heart comes from love lost, the untimely death of a loved one, the disappointment of a child's behavior, or the demise of a dear dream, you must stretch out your hands and give it over to God. The closer you hold the pain to your breast, babying, nursing, and rehearsing the offense, the disappointment, the travesty that has occurred, the longer it will take to heal. First Peter 5:6,7 says:

> "Humble yourselves, therefore, under God's mighty hand, that he may lift you up in due time. Cast all your anxiety on him because he cares for you."

While we're not able to lift ourselves, God is there to lift us. Casting our cares on the Lord also means that we should release our ideas of how God should remedy the situation. To decide how God should champion our cause is actually to revel in pride. It is actually exalting our needs above the unknown needs of our offender. Therefore, we must release the pain and the decision of how God should deal with the pain.

Don't hide your pain. Humble yourself, reach out, and give it to the Lord. Stop coddling it. Stop talking about it. The more you cradle your pain, the louder it will cry. The more you talk about it, the more upset you will get. Replaying the old tape over and over only reignites your initial feelings. So stop stirring up old stuff. Let go of the spoon. Stretch out your hands. Allow the Lord to take your pain and restore your heart. Embrace the principle of release.

It Hurts So Good

Let's talk about why we cling to pain. I must ask you the question voiced in an old Hebrew proverb: "Is the pain dear to you?" If yes, why? Has it moved beyond the point of being a heartfelt emotion to becoming a tool for getting attention? Has it become a device to manipulate the hand of God? He will not be moved by tears alone. He is moved by the principles of His own word. If the other person is in the wrong, you can be sure that He will move on your behalf, *but*—and here's the part we don't like—*in His own time*. Remember, His ultimate goal is to bring us all into right standing with Himself. Only after that has been accomplished can we be in a fruitful relationship with anyone else. Only then will those who hurt us be able to see and acknowledge the error of their ways and make a change for the better. Our relational skills are only as well developed as our relationship with God. This is truly revealing. Your ability to release another individual will depend greatly on the depth of your connection with the only true Lover of your soul.

Still, we cling to our suffering, glorying in it. We settle into it. Pain becomes a comforting habit—the martyr complex. The one who has offended us should feel *sooo* bad if he knew how his behavior has affected us! He should just be writhing in agony too. Others should feel our pain when they see us and cluck sympathetically over our sad state of affairs. We deserve all the attention we can get at this point. We have been victimized. Though this may seem to be a good reason to wallow in our sorrows, it is actually a self-serving reason, one that is not profitable for our hearts. It is, I'm sorry to say, another form of pride. When we parade our pain in front of others to the extreme, we are literally saying, "Look at what I've endured. Shouldn't I get the credit for suffering so well?" We take pride in someone saying, "Oh, it's been three years, and she still hasn't recovered. She must have really loved him. How horrible of him not to appreciate her love!" It is still turning the attention toward ourselves. It is a form of self-indulgence that is designed to position us in a twisted sort of way as lord of our situation. After all, we reason, it's all about us. Yet, the only thing we should be happy to suffer for is the purposes of God.

> "In bringing many sons to **glory**, it was fitting that God, for whom and through whom everything exists, should make the author of their salvation perfect through **suffering**" (Hebrews 2:10, emphasis mine).

> "But how is it to your credit if you receive a beating for doing wrong and endure it? But if you suffer for doing good and you endure it, this is commendable before God" (1 Peter 2:20).

We are certainly not greater than Jesus, who suffered for our sake without complaining. Think of Him who was rejected and despised time and time again. And what was His crime? Simply loving and being willing to die for those who would not appreciate it. And still *even He* had to let go, to release those He had come to love and to save. After all, they were free agents. Imagine His heartbreak as He stood looking out over Jerusalem, weeping.

> "O **Jerusalem**, **Jerusalem**, you who kill the prophets and stone those sent to you, how often I have longed to gather your children together, as a **hen** gathers her chicks under her wings, but you were not willing!" (Luke 13:34, emphasis mine).

You are not alone in having your heart insulted, your love rejected, your good intentions evil-spoken of. And yet you must let the offense go. The inability to let go reveals a heart that is filled with unforgiveness. Yet what we fail to realize is that the more we cling to the offense and the more we hold the person in unforgiveness, the longer we are held in bondage ourselves. It stops us from moving on. We are stuck to what we cling to. Remember the fable about Tar Baby? Brer Fox was upset about being outwitted by Brer Rabbit and, knowing his nature very well, laid a very clever trap for him. He positioned a little wooden doll covered with tar in the middle of the road, hid himself, and waited for Brer Rabbit to happen by. Well, of course, soon enough here comes Brer Rabbit. He stops to say hello to Tar Baby, who says nothing back. The refusal of Tar Baby to acknowledge him miffs Brer Rabbit to no end, so he hauls off and whacks Tar Baby across the head. To his dismay, he finds his hand is stuck to the tar! This simply incenses him further. He rails and threatens Tar Baby with another punch if he doesn't let go of his hand. Of course, Tar Baby says nothing, so Brer Rabbit socks him again and finds his other hand stuck to Tar Baby as well. This is followed by a head butt to the unresponsive Tar Baby. By now, Brer Fox can no longer contain his mirth; he leaps from his hiding place to taunt his helpless victim, who is writhing in self-imposed bondage.

Confession Is Good for the Soul

Get the picture? It's true that hurt people hurt other people, but my question is this: Who hurts the most? Those who refuse to take the open door the Lord provides to healing. Holding on to offense keeps us bound to our offender. We cannot let go. I believe the greatest part of the problem is our refusal to state how we really feel about the person and what he's done to us. In our minds, good little Christians would never dare mutter the words, "I really hate so-and-so for that." Yet the Bible is filled with godly men who cried out to God to commit horrible acts of vengeance for their sakes. David did it. The prophets did it. And yet we take the polite route, stifling our pain and our real feelings. We sit, we stew, we seethe. We wait to be healed while never exposing the real wound. We'd rather get an ulcer than be honest. After all, if we're really saved, we shouldn't have such emotions.

Let It All Hang Out

I find it interesting that in every case where people in the Bible asked God to do something horrible to their offender, He never chastised them for voicing their sentiments. And what sentiments they were! "Destroy and divide their tongues!...let death seize them and let them go down quick into hell!" "Consume them in wrath." "Let shame come upon them...leave them to wander like dogs...." Hey, they might as well have yelled, "Off with their heads!" They were serious! Yet through all the railing, ranting, and raving, God listened, let them get it off their chests, and then set about the business of healing their hearts and dealing with their enemies. God can only work with what we acknowledge. Remember that. Someone once said that genuine forgiveness is only possible when there has been a genuine articulation of the hurt. So, in other words, spit it out!

Medically speaking, we know that wounds do not heal until they are exposed to air. To keep them covered makes them susceptible to infection. And you never know until the bandage falls off and you smell the wound. Recently, I was mortified to feel my temperature rising as I recounted the history of a relationship that had ended over nine years ago. As I shared with a friend what had happened, I heard my voice escalating. The frown of concern that crossed my friend's face did not cause me to pull myself in check. I was too far gone in my dramatic delivery. "You know, you need to deal with that," she said. To which I replied, "No, I don't, I've already dealt with it; it's behind me. I just got annoyed when I thought about it. You know, he never apologized for what he did to me even though I know intellectually that he feels bad about it." My understanding friend replied, "I know, you're right. He *does* owe you an apology, but he might be incapable of giving it. At any rate, you still have to free yourself, even if he never says he's sorry." By now we had made our way to the elevator of the hotel we were in. As we waited for the door to open, I said, "It's just not fair..." To which my friend replied, "Michelle, you need to get this out once and for all. I tell you what, after this session [we were both speaking at a conference] I am going to sit and listen and just let you vent." That's as far as she got before the floodgates opened and I dashed to my room to recover from the sobs that seemed to come from my toes, talking to myself all the while that I needed to suck it up. After all, I was a speaker—I couldn't afford to fall apart when I had a roomful of women waiting for a message of hope from me! Needless to say, I was not anxious to visit that place of pain again, so I avoided my friend for the rest of the afternoon. But God got me that night.

As I sat listening to another one of my friends giving an inspirational message in the evening session, the truth of what my friend had said to me earlier that day snuck up on me like a velvet-covered hammer. She was talking about surrendering the unpleasant, unpalatable things in our lives to Jesus, about giving Him the things you think that no one would want. These are the things that He blesses, then breaks, then serves to others to strengthen them and glorify Himself. We just don't like to bring them out into the open and offer them up because they don't look so pretty. "Let Him have it," she said. "Only then can He make it something that can be used for His glory and your good. What if the little boy who had the barley loaves that fed the crowd at the Sermon on the Mount had decided that no one would want to eat his hard, pithy little loaves? But he gave them up, and Jesus fed the multitude with them. A miracle came out of those meager offerings. What do you need to give to Jesus? The good, the bad, the ugly—why not give it all to Him and let Him bless it, break it, and give it to nourish others?" I sat there weeping, offering the Lord my anger, my pain, my unfor-giveness. I confessed my state of resentment. It felt so good to pour it all out before Him. Yes, I was ashamed to have been harboring those things. But you know what? I never felt the Lord correcting me; I only felt His compas-sion as He listened to me pouring out my grief. And then His comfort came and I was free—free to thank Him, free to share this with you in this chapter so that you can know you're not alone. Others have been on the path that you take, and there is comfort in the arms of Jesus as you let Him know exactly where you are. Like balloons in the wind that disappear above the clouds, our distress disap-pears when we release it into the hands of our loving, caring God.

Why do you need to forgive? You need to forgive for your own sake. You do not hold the other person prisoner with your silent resentment, your silent punishment, or your callous snubbing. You only bind yourself. Why do you need to forgive? Because you yourself need forgive-ness. To hold others hostage to their offenses is to put God in remembrance of your offense toward another.

"'Therefore, the kingdom of heaven is like a king who wanted to settle accounts with his servants. As he began the settlement, a man who owed him ten thousand talents was brought to him. Since he was not able to pay, the master ordered that he and his wife and his children and all that he had be sold to repay the debt. The servant fell on his knees before him. "Be patient with me," he begged, "and I will pay back everything." The servant's master took pity on him, cancelled the debt and let him go. But when that servant went out, he found one of his fellow servants who owed him a hundred denarii. He grabbed him and began to choke him. "Pay back what you owe me!" he demanded. His fellow servant fell to his knees and begged him, "Be patient with me, and I will pay you back." But he refused. Instead, he went off and had the man thrown into prison until he could pay the debt. When the other servants saw what had happened, they were greatly distressed and went and told their master everything that had happened. Then the master called the servant in. "You wicked servant," he said, "I cancelled all that debt of yours because you begged me to. Shouldn't you have had mercy on your fellow servant just as I had on you?" In anger his master turned him over to the jailers to be tortured, until he should pay back all he owed. This is how my heavenly Father will treat each of you unless you forgive your brother from your heart'" (Matthew 18:23-35).

As they say, "What goes around comes around." There is no such thing as just getting over it. Offenses must be pulled out in the open and dealt with at the foot of the cross. Ignoring your feelings is a bad joke that will eventually backfire. Trust me, all those pressed-down hurts and disappointments will resurface at a most inopportune moment—usually when you're on the brink of receiving a great blessing that the devil wants you to blow. So, please don't give him anything to use. Rubbing your pain in the face of your offender only sets you up for more rejection. Bitterness is just not worth it. The wear and tear on your soul is too much to bear. It keeps you from moving forward. In my own life, unforgiveness has ruptured my ability to trust others who sought to get close to me. How many valuable opportunities for rich relationships have I allowed to slip through my fingers simply because I was stuck? I won't know until eternity. But for now I know that my own emotional stubbornness has cost me while I dwelt on what I felt was owed to me. I failed to acknowledge the truth that I am owed nothing in this world. Jesus paid it all and my rights are now hidden in Him.

> "**Forgive** us our debts, as we also have forgiven our debtors....For if you **forgive** men when they sin against you, your heavenly Father will also **forgive** you. But if you do not **forgive** men their sins, your Father will not **forgive** your sins" (Matthew 6:12,14,15, emphasis mine).

The bottom line is that when it comes to offense, everyone is operating out of where they've been. Without the help of Christ, they can do no more than that. Whether out of ignorance or purposeful action, we are all propelled on our courses by the baggage we carry until we deposit those cumbersome loads at the feet of Jesus. A friend recently told me something that caused me to take a deep pause. He said, "We've been taught that Jesus was insulted, beaten, and crucified for our sakes, and yet we feel we don't have to take anything from anybody. If the servant is not greater than the master, then how do we reconcile that?" Speaking of things that make you go hmm…! If we are dead and our lives are hidden in Christ, we must allow Him to shield us from the blows that the world inflicts upon us. We must live offensively, not defensively. We should not be so horribly thrown every time someone else hurts us. Our expectations should be placed in God alone. Man is fallible and will offend. Staying in the spirit, close to the Father, prepares us for things to come so that we are not leveled by them. Jesus was never surprised at the things that people did to Him. He expected their behavior and tried to train the disciples in the same manner.

> "Then said he unto the disciples, 'It is impossible but that offenses **will come**: but woe unto him, through whom they **come**!'" (Luke 17:1 KJV, emphasis mine).

Another translation says, "It is inevitable that the stumbling blocks will come…." Another says, "The things that will cause people to sin will come…." If we know this to be true, then we should not be surprised when others hurt and disappoint us. Jesus is saying, "Expect it so that you can deal with it properly." Part of being able to deal with it properly is knowing that God does not take what you go through lightly. He intends to chasten the person who is in the wrong. He collects your tears in a bottle, according to Psalm 56:8, and does not dismiss the cry of even one. He rises to your defense based on the pain that you endure unjustly, not on your cries for vengeance. It is important to grasp this. Whether in pain or in happiness, in victory or in victimization, we are called to imitate Christ and to release our offenses back to the only One who is able to deal with them fairly. And in that we find our own sweet release and healing.

> "But he was pierced for **our transgressions**, he was crushed for **our iniquities;** the punishment that brought us peace was upon him, and by his wounds we are healed" (Isaiah 53:5, emphasis mine).

> "Jesus said, '**Father**, **forgive them**; for they know not what they are doing'" (Luke 23:34, emphasis mine).

> "Blessed are the merciful: for they will be shown **mercy**" (Matthew 5:7, emphasis mine).

My dear friend, carefully consider what it is that you need from God and be willing to give in order to receive.

Can you talk about the circumstances of the offense without getting upset? If not, what upsets you most?

Do you secretly hope that your offender will hear of your pain? If yes, why?

What reaction would you like him to have?

What is your reaction when you hear of something good happening to him? Does it cause you to question God's fairness?

How do you think God should settle the matter? What do you think He should do to the one who has hurt you? How would this affect that person's salvation?

Do you believe God has a plan for you?

Do you feel that His plan for you has been circumvented because of what has happened to you? How much power does any human being have over God's designed destiny?

How do we give our power away? Have you done that in this case?

Do you believe that God is aware of your pain and wants to do something about it?

What must you do to put yourself in a position to be blessed?

Is your state of unforgiveness keeping you from communicating with God? Do you feel free to voice your desires to Him? Do you believe that He will answer you?

Do you believe that God is just? What does that mean? Do you trust His sovereign decisions? What makes you hesitate to release the situation to Him? What do you think He will do? Not do? Why?

Do you believe that He will work on your behalf and for your good?

Do you believe that God is on your side? What does that mean?

Do you believe that He cares about your pain? Can He heal you? Will you allow Him to?

What will it take for you to release your pain to Him? Do you trust Him with it? Are you weary of it yet?

Be blatantly honest with God about how you feel right now. Make a confession of release.

The Spirit of the Sovereign LORD is on me, because the LORD has anointed me to preach good news to the poor. He has sent me to bind up the brokenhearted...to comfort all who mourn, and provide for those who grieve in Zion—to bestow on them a crown of beauty instead of ashes, the oil of gladness instead of mourning, and a garment of praise instead of a spirit of despair. They will be called oaks of righteousness, a planting of the LORD for the display of his splendor. They will rebuild the ancient ruins and restore the places long devastated; they will renew the ruined cities that have been devastated for generations.

Isaiah 61:1-4

7

Rebuilding the Temple

Now that you've gotten everything out of your system, you're probably wondering what to do next. The phantom pain of the other person's presence remains, making you feel strange. What exactly does one do in the silence after a storm? A time when all is eerily calm? You simply wait and allow the light to settle around you. There comes a time after releasing all when you must let sleeping dogs lie. Don't talk about it anymore. Don't allow others to talk about it either. The devil will always send someone in the name of comfort to keep you stuck in the same spot. Practice silence. This is when God speaks. He comes with loving instructions on where to go from here.

It is very tempting to look at the shambles of your relationship and feel weary, utterly hopeless, with no signs of healing in sight. The thought of reconstructing your life is enough to make you want to go back to bed. Yet forge on you must. You must begin to pick up the pieces and rebuild your life. The Master Builder stands ready to assist you. Simply put your hand in His and follow where He leads.

When the prophet Nehemiah was sent the news of how the walls of Jerusalem lay in ruins, his countenance fell and great sadness overwhelmed him. It seemed an impossible task to restore them to glory, yet God touched the heart of his master, King Artaxerxes of Persia, to release him to go and rebuild the walls. The king not only commissioned Nehemiah to go, but also gave him what he needed to do the job. So Nehemiah went forth with a firm determination to restore the place that was dear to his heart. This he shared with a select few.

> "Then I said to them, 'You see the trouble we are in: Jerusalem lies in ruins, and its gates have been burned with fire. Come, let us rebuild the wall of Jerusalem, and we will no longer be in disgrace'"
> (Nehemiah 2:17).

Truly, the walls of your heart have been leveled. You are vulnerable and open to the attack of the enemy, but God is sending you reinforcements. All that is required of you is the resolve to rebuild. Now, understand and know that simply because you decide to take your life back and pull yourself together, you should not take it for granted that things will go smoothly. Mm-mm, the enemy of your soul will not be amused by your new attitude. He will fight you tooth and nail. He will ridicule you, taunt you. And he will make you feel uncertain that you can complete the task. If he sees that this tactic isn't working, he will offer to help you. His rationale? If he is involved in your rebuilding process, he will make sure that the foundation is so shaky that it tumbles again. Believe me, he is not interested in your health and welfare. But you must take the stance of Nehemiah.

> "I answered them by saying, 'The God of heaven will give us success. We his servants will start rebuilding, but as for you, you have no share in Jerusalem or any claim or historic right to it'" (Nehemiah 2:20).

Picking Up the Pieces

It is true that God will be your partner and grant you complete healing. He will take your heart piece by piece and put it back together, each piece fitly joined together, stronger than before. Some days will be better than others. Such is the process of working through grieving. The enemy will send people and situations to distract you and throw you off your course. You'll receive news of what the other person is doing or saying. You'll hear doubts and fears expressed about your future. All of these things are designed to slow down your progress and rob you of your healing. But you must stand your ground and continue on, trusting God to keep you.

> "They were all trying to frighten us, thinking, 'Their hands will get too weak for the work, and it will not be completed.' But I prayed, 'Now strengthen my hands'" (Nehemiah 6:9).

> "Sanballat and Geshem sent me this message: 'Come, let us meet together in one of the villages on the plain of Ono.' But they were scheming to

> harm me; so I sent messengers to them with this reply: 'I am carrying on a great project and cannot go down. Why should the work stop while I leave it and go down to you?'" (Nehemiah 6:2).

You've got to possess an immovable resolve to complete your restoration. Upsets will come as you begin to sort through the rubble. You see, Nehemiah and the others didn't use all new timber and stone. They used some of the stones that had been charred and shattered when the city had been overthrown. They discerned what they could use and threw out the rest, and the enemy came to taunt, point out, and ridicule their efforts.

> "...and in the presence of his [Sanballat's] associates and the army of Samaria, he said, 'What are those feeble Jews doing? Will they restore their wall? Will they offer sacrifices? Will they finish in a day? Can they bring the stones back to life from those heaps of rubble—burned as they are?'" (Nehemiah 4:2).

Can you, indeed? In this case your past pain can be your friend, giving you the wisdom you need to rebuild your world. Yes, there is still usable substance from your past experience. Use it. It may not look so good, but dust it off and use it; it still has worth. Don't throw out the baby with the bathwater. Take your time, and do it well. Don't let your calendar be a factor. Don't use it to measure your progress. God is not in a hurry when it comes to the healing process. Take it one day at a time. Give your stones to God and let Him breathe life into them. Keep the sweet spirit you had before. Keep the hope you had in love before. Keep the faith you had before. These are the reusable stones. I'm sure you have more.

Now as you begin to pick the stones up, God is going to show you something about each one. He will show you how it was mishandled. He might show you how it was left open to attack. He will also show you the beauty of each stone. He will reveal His word and will concerning every stone in your life. And with every stone that you lift, He will ask you to give it to Him as a sacrifice. This can be difficult, but we must pass this way. Some of these words might cut deeply. Your contrition might be great as you review your own mistakes. Your wounds might open afresh, but don't stop at this stage of development. Allow those tears to cleanse you, but don't let them dampen your spirit.

> "Then Nehemiah the governor, Ezra the priest and scribe, and the Levites who were instructing the people said to them all, 'This day is sacred to the LORD your God. Do not mourn or weep.' For all the people had been weeping as they listened to the words of the Law. Nehemiah said, 'Go and enjoy choice food and sweet drinks, and send some to those who have nothing prepared. This day is sacred to our Lord. Do not grieve, for the joy of the LORD is your strength.' The Levites calmed all the people, saying, 'Be still, for this is a sacred day. Do not grieve'" (Nehemiah 8:9-11).

Beginning Again

Remember that saying "Today is the first day of the rest of your life"? Well, this is it! I am so happy to know that God is not the God of the second chance. He is the God of as many chances as we need to get it right. We fail, we fall, we hurt. He is there at every turn, while the devil berates us with everything we've done wrong—how undesirable we are, how unloveable and hopeless we are, how we'll never get it right. But Jesus comes along and says, "That's not what I see when I look at you." And on that note, He begins to repair the breaches in the walls of our hearts, gently speaking words of love and kindness, sealing the spaces between with His precious Holy Spirit. Oh, thank God for His wonderful grace, His indulgent heart, His unending compassion! Indeed, this is not a day to grieve; it is a day of new beginnings!

He urges you to eat and gain your strength so that you may be joyful. What should you eat?

> "Why spend money on what is not bread, and your labor on what does not satisfy? Listen, listen to me, and **eat** what is **good**, and your soul will delight in the richest of fare" (Isaiah 55:2, emphasis mine).

> "Man does not live on **bread alone** but on every word that comes from the mouth of the LORD" (Deuteronomy 8:3, emphasis mine).

I believe that you should eat on three levels. First, you must spiritually partake of God's word. You must erase every lie of the enemy and replace each one with God's truth. Forget what everybody else thinks. What does *God* think of you? What does He desire for your life? This is your time to cling to His garments and refuse to let go until He blesses you. Stay in His presence until you hear a clear word from Him, a word that will rebuild your spirit. Ask Him to put you in remembrance of the covenant that He made with you. Write it down and make it plain to yourself so that you can walk in the assurance that you have a direct promise from God concerning you. You are important to Him, and He has a word that will heal you and equip you to be free.

The story continues in Nehemiah that the people built shelters or tents on top of their houses in which to live while they observed the Festival of Tabernacles, a time set aside for worshipping the Lord. If I might spiritualize this a bit for the benefit of making my point, it would be this: Cover your head. Do not leave it uncovered for the enemy to plant thoughts and pluck the seed of hope and renewal that the Lord has planted. Take the word that has been given to you and set aside the time to worship Him, anticipating the complete manifestation of your healing. Yet in all of this, stay open enough for God to do His work in you. You see, the tent was not as secure as the house; it was merely a covering against the worst of the elements. It was not fortified to keep everything out. We must leave room for God to work through the fabric of our entire being.

Second, you need to eat physical food, to build up your strength. Don't go overboard now. But do take care of your physical body. If your body is suffering and not getting what it needs, it will affect your emotions. Build up your immune system and your resistance so that you can stand against the attacks that can threaten your health when you are assaulted with depression and apprehension. When your resistance is built up and you are physically strong, you have a greater capacity to persevere.

Third, eat from life again. Begin to do something. Eat from the trees that God has put around you. Get involved in the things of interest you ignored during your trial. Get out. Mix and mingle. Discover new friends or rediscover some old ones. Find new interests. Fill your world with things that complete you and expand your horizons. Do something you never did before. Trying something new can be invigorating. Staying in the same old routine only reminds you of all the holes that now seem vacant. Fill them with something before the enemy finds something to fill them with.

Now, after the people had built themselves back up and regained their strength, they fasted (see Nehemiah chapter 9) and returned to hear the word of the Lord. Sometimes you're not ready for everything in one big dose. God knows that. He will wait for you to regain your strength; then He'll tackle some of the issues He knows you are now ready to deal with. Back to the story of Nehemiah. The people received God's word, confessed their sins, and then turned to worship and praise the Lord. They rehearsed His greatness in the assembly and listed His attributes to remind themselves of His goodness. Then they recommitted themselves back to Him. They made a fresh covenant to serve the Lord, and they signed it. They walked the full length of the walls that had been restored and dedicated the gates, the people, and the wall to the Lord. Proceeding onward to the Temple, they sang and worshipped the Lord so loudly that their joy was heard far away. And, last but not least, they purified the Temple and expelled all the enemies of the Lord out of the assembly. Nehemiah then took measures to preserve the sanctity of the Sabbath.

Reoccupying the Land

What does all of this mean to us in our restoration process? Well, as we seek to get totally free, we must deal with the people who are the hardest to deal with—ourselves. Crucifying our flesh to really hear what God is saying is even harder. We must be willing to examine ourselves and take responsibility for our own mistakes, should God reveal any to us. Taking stock of all we've said and done is a major building block because it paves the way for us to cash in on life lessons that will enrich our lives from this day forward if we pay heed to them. Yes, confession is good for the soul. We should praise God for the privilege of being able to come into His presence and leave our mess there. Sometimes we are horrified by what we see and He reveals. But as we see the blood of Jesus wash these things away right before our eyes, we can only worship Him for His goodness and mercy.

Sometimes, in the hard places, we forget His former mercies. But it is good to revisit them, to take stock of how far He has brought us, to remember the things He has delivered us from in the past. After taking joyful inventory, you should be in the mood to recommit your life, your heart, your everything, back to Him. After all, He has proven Himself to be faithful.

Make a new covenant with God. Covenant to go to another level with Him, deeper into your relationship. Then walk out your restoration. Occupy every inch of it, and leave no part of it unoccupied for the enemy to snatch back. Secure your deliverance by rendering a loud praise that others hear as you commit even your newfound freedom back to the Lord. Purify yourself and get rid of anything that will displease the Lord and rob you of your restoration—negative associates, little unnecessary comments, imaginations and habits that can stop the flow of blessing. Sanctify the Sabbath in your heart. By that, I mean rest. Stop striving. Stop working to make things happen, and rest in Him. Bask in the knowledge that you have come out and your land is now secure, your temple rebuilt, your heart finally whole.

When you stand in the rubble of your situation, what do you see?

What can you salvage from the pile of your circumstances? Which stones can you use? How can you use them?

What does the enemy whisper to you as you examine your fate? Is it the truth?

What part is a lie? What is God's truth about your situation?

Who are the people the enemy is using in your life to reinforce your pain? How do they do this?

What boundaries can you set to ensure your healing?

What do you fear about the future? What doubts do you have concerning your ability to move on from where you are? Why do you have them?

What is God saying to you? What Scripture has He given you to meditate on? What do you get out of it to apply to yourself?

What do you feel you need to confess to God in light of what He has shared with you?

Make a list of former blessings He has given you, and worship Him.

Write a prayer of recommitment to the Lord and make a new covenant with Him. Sign and date it.

Now make a confession concerning your restoration and what God has done for you in your present situation.

Make a list of purification. What things do you need to get rid of in order to secure your healing? What thoughts? Habits? Conversations? Confessions?

What things have you still been working hard at? What have you been trying to make happen?

How do you feel when it doesn't work out the way in which you intended? Was your plan God-directed or you-directed?

Now sanctify the Sabbath in your heart. Write a list of all that you are leaving in His care, and rest in Him.

Anyone who listens to the word but does not do what it says is like a man who looks at his face in a mirror and, after looking at himself, goes away and immediately forgets what he looks like. But the man who looks intently into the perfect law that gives freedom, and continues to do this, not forgetting what he has heard, but doing it—he will be blessed in what he does.

James 1:23-25

8

The Woman in the Mirror

Take a look at yourself. What do you see? Lean into the mirror and look into your own eyes. What do they tell you? Have you grown wiser through it all? What lessons do your eyes give away? Is there a new grace upon you? There should be. If the enemy of your soul has told you that you were a fool, don't believe him. Everyone makes mistakes. Everyone suffers heartbreak. But only fools refuse to learn from their experiences. Fools have very specific earmarks, in God's eyes.

> "Resentment kills a **fool**, and envy slays the simple" (Job 5:2, emphasis mine).

> "The **fool** says in his heart, 'There is no God'" (Psalm 53:1, emphasis mine).

135

> "...whoever spreads slander is a **fool**" (Proverbs 10:18, emphasis mine).
>
> "...a **fool** is hotheaded and reckless" (Proverbs 14:16, emphasis mine).
>
> "A **fool** spurns his father's discipline..." (Proverbs 15:5, emphasis mine).
>
> "...every **fool** is quick to quarrel" (Proverbs 20:3, emphasis mine).
>
> "...a **fool** repeats his folly" (Proverbs 26:11, emphasis mine).
>
> "...the **fool** lacks sense and shows everyone how stupid he is" (Ecclesiastes 10:3, emphasis mine).

Well, there it is! By now I'm sure you've released any anger and resentment you may be harboring and stopped talking negatively about the one who has offended you. You've refused to embrace unbelief because you know it will not be a kind friend. Faith is the only thing that will bring you out of where you are. You've been open to the correction of your Heavenly Father as well as to wise earthly counsel and purposed not to revisit this place; therefore, you are not a fool.

The Path of Wisdom

All wise people embrace the lessons that their pain teaches them. Of course, in many cases, the offense was not our fault, but still we must be open to the fact that some parts of what took place could be ours to account for. It is always important to take inventory and clear our slates to make room for a new equation. Heartbreak comes in many forms besides the romantic, and many examples can be applied to your situation in theory.

Joseph, for instance, was heartbroken by the unjust betrayal of his own brothers because of their jealousy toward him. But even here, there was a lesson to be learned. Perhaps his quickness to reveal his dreams contributed to his hardship. Yet God used it to work out a more glorious plan. In the end, a more mature Joseph pondered things before he spoke, moved more carefully, and made a very wise observance upon being reconciled with his brothers.

> "You intended to harm me, but God intended it for good to accomplish what is now being done, the saving of many lives" (Genesis 50:20).

Joseph went on to admit that he had grown and become a better person because of his ordeal. The impulsive, spoiled little boy was replaced by a sober man who moved with prudence, always weighing his decisions in the light of God's purposes versus his own personal desires. He yielded to the sovereign hand of God and refused to be bitter about the things that had happened to him, seeing God's wisdom in the midst of his circumstances. He pressed past the pain to see the bigger picture. In my own case, I know the many failed relationships I've endured have given birth to my ministry. The lessons I've learned and shared have saved many from imitating my mistakes. God has taken my trials and turned them into a blessing for many.

> "The second son he named Ephraim and said, 'It is because God has made me **fruitful** in the land of my suffering'" (Genesis 41:52, emphasis mine).

Your trial is an opportunity to become fruitful. You can decide to allow the companions of sorrow and suffering to be transformed into grace and glory in your life. The other option is far too unpleasant.

Job was a man who was heartbroken over the overwhelming loss of everything he possessed—houses, livestock, family—and yet he was diligent about clinging to his faith.

> "I know that my Redeemer lives, and that in the end he will stand upon the earth. And after my skin has been destroyed, yet in my flesh I will see God…" (Job 19:25,26).

In other words, all of this is temporal and unimportant. What is important will remain; I will see God. Perhaps life has not been kind, but that does not negate the presence and the faithfulness of God. Wow! And Job was able to say this while being beaten down by friends who did not understand his plight. His wife had urged him to curse God and die before disappearing out of the story. Job endured heartbreak piled on top of heartbreak, but he clung to God and—get this—prayed for those knuckleheaded friends of his! Have you prayed yet for the one who offended you? Have you chosen to bless him and not curse him? Praying for the one who hurt you is an important ingredient in the forgiveness process. Job knew this was the answer to his breakthrough. He sowed seeds for his own restoration as he prayed for his friends. And he prayed for them because in the end he could not fault them for the things they said. He realized that he too had been shortsighted in his understanding of God and the way in which He deals with us.

> "Then Job replied to the LORD: 'I know that you can do all things; no plan of yours can be thwarted. You asked, "Who is this that obscures my counsel

without knowledge?" Surely I spoke of things I did not understand, things too wonderful for me to know. You said, "Listen now, and I will speak; I will question you, and you shall answer me." My ears had heard of you but now my eyes have seen you. Therefore I despise myself and repent in dust and ashes'" (Job 42:1-6).

Indeed, who can figure God out? Who can say why He allows bad things to happen to good people? Two things we can be sure of—in the end His restoration is sure, and important lessons can be learned. So many of us can second the motion so profoundly uttered by Job: "I had heard of you, but now I've seen you in action for myself. And how little did I know!" It is sad but true—most of the time, it takes a good trial to turn our attention back to the Lord. Only then do we get the opportunity to see a side of Him we never saw before—that is, if we truly seek to see Him move in our midst. He comes and shows Himself strong on our behalf, revealing His purposes, putting our fears to shame. As most know, Job was doubly blessed at the end his life. God restored all that he had lost and more.

Seeing the Bigger Picture

Beloved, we cannot see the whole picture. I cannot tell you why you are going through what you are going through except to say that it all will fit somehow, some way, into God's supreme kingdom agenda. He trusted you to make it through this. As in the case of Job, I believe that sometimes conversations held in heaven get us in trouble here on earth. The enemy comes to prove to God that you are not all that He says you're cracked up to be. You must prove him wrong. Shame the devil by being a good and faithful servant to the Most High in spite of what He allows. This too shall pass. It always does.

Naomi, Orpah, and Ruth were three women who suffered the heartbreak of losing their husbands. How differently they responded! Ruth remained gracious and loving, willing to follow her mother-in-law to a strange country to care for her. Orpah decided to remain where she had always been and nurse her sorrows. I find it interesting that we never hear anything else about her life. And there was Naomi (which means "pleasant"), who proclaimed loudly that her name should be changed to Mara (which means "bitter") because she decided that the Lord had dealt bitterly with her. She had a serious pity party upon arriving back in Bethlehem. Though we never read about it in Scripture, I'm sure she repented for her words after she had seen the hand and purposes of God unfold. Ruth met a wealthy man in Naomi's family by the name of Boaz and married him. And Naomi was not only blessed with a wonderful, kind son-in-law, but also with a comfortable existence and a grandchild who would be the great-grandfather of the king of Israel, David. And all of this happened because her grievous situation forced her to move into the position to receive greater provision from the Lord.

Perhaps your trial, your pain, and your disappointment have been designed to move you from where you are and put you in the position to receive a greater blessing! God moves in mysterious ways His wonders to perform. We know that priceless pearls are born from a grain of sand irritating the delicate insides of an oyster. In its fight to do away with the source of pain, the oyster produces a pearl in the midst of its struggle. Truly, every setback is an opportunity to spring forward. So lean into it and allow its pressure to propel you to the next level. Like the mother who holds her baby in her arms after enduring much travail, we can rest assured that there is a reward at the end of our labor.

> "Not only so, but we also rejoice in our sufferings, because we know that suffering produces perseverance; perseverance, character; and character, hope. And hope does not disappoint us, because God has poured out his love into our hearts by the Holy Spirit, whom he has given us" (Romans 5:3-5).

Another translation says that hope does not make us ashamed. Yes, it takes away our shame, our fear of what we look like to others who watched our situation unfold. We know that God will come through for us. Therefore, we will turn to Him, sit at His feet, learn more of Him, and ask Him for the wisdom we need to continue our journey. But lessons are not lessons learned unless they are applied. We are encouraged in Proverbs to get understanding in the midst of all the other things we gain in life.

> "Blessed is the man who finds wisdom, the man who gains **understanding**..." (Proverbs 3:13, emphasis mine).

> "Get wisdom, **get understanding**; do not forget my words or swerve from them" (Proverbs 4:5, emphasis mine).

> "Wisdom is supreme; therefore get wisdom. Though it cost all you have, **get understanding**" (Proverbs 4:7, emphasis mine).

> "He who gets wisdom loves his own soul; he who cherishes **understanding** prospers" (Proverbs 19:8, emphasis mine).

"Buy the truth and do not sell it; get wisdom, discipline and **understanding**" (Proverbs 23:23, emphasis mine).

Get wisdom, get knowledge, get understanding. I like to call them the dynamic trio. We all know an educated fool. This is someone who has a lot of knowledge but has no understanding; therefore, he does not conduct himself wisely. Get it? The knowledge you gain must be broken down to a practical understanding so that you can walk in wisdom. You must be willing to assess past mistakes and learn from them, purposing not to repeat them again. Walking in wisdom is what helps us to avoid the enemy's snares, the counterfeits that slip into our lives and lead us captive because of our desires.

For those of us who have suffered romantically, when we look back we see the little red flags. The warnings. Friends or parents said things that we didn't want to hear. We chose to ignore their admonition, but now we have to admit that what they said was true. Some of you would quietly hang your head in shame and admit that you knew you had no business with the likes of this man, but you hoped that by your good example he would change. However, he did not. And upon his exit from your life, he wreaked havoc on your heart, your spirit, and your emotions. Others of you are sitting in shock because you cannot believe that a man who had given you every indication that he was a sold-out, born-again believer has misused you worse than the men you have experienced in the secular world. This brings to mind a Scripture I overlooked for years because I had relegated it to the category of men in the world. To my surprise, God revealed to me that He was speaking of men in the church! Take a look:

"But realize this, that in the last days difficult times will come. For men will be lovers of self, lovers of money, boastful, arrogant, revilers, disobedient to parents, ungrateful, unholy, unloving, irreconcilable, malicious gossips, without self-control, brutal, haters of good, treacherous, reckless, conceited, lovers of pleasure rather than lovers of God; holding to a form of godliness, although they have denied its power; and avoid such men as these. For among them are those who enter into households and captivate weak women weighed down with sins, led on by various impulses, always learning and never able to come to the knowledge of the truth" (2 Timothy 3:1-7 NASB).

Whoa! That is heavy-duty. There are those who will have a form of godliness but do not feel the need to hold themselves accountable to God for how they treat you. They are consumed by the cares of this world and only give lip service to God. A man who has not embraced an intimate relationship with God and entered into true covenant with him will never be able to commit to you as he should. If you don't walk in wisdom, you will not be able to discern the wolf in sheep's clothing's presence in your life.

So many of us jump at the opportunity to have a relationship. Because we have been waiting for so long, we fail to stop and ask God to reveal the person to us. We don't want to know, though we already have an inkling. Because of the Holy Spirit who abides in us, we are never truly ignorant. We fail to ask God what our assignment is concerning this person. We've already decided what slot we want this person to fit into in our lives. Well, God might have other plans that will save us a lot of heartache. Perhaps He would have us walk as a sister and an example in this man's life and not be involved with him at all, but no, we are off and running to the races. We become silly, weak women because we are laden down with the desire to have someone in our lives. Though we intellectually know certain things, we fail to grasp an understanding of what those things could cost us long term. Therefore, we proceed without caution or wisdom. We learn from the last romantic catastrophe and then throw that information to the wind when the next opportunity at love comes along. We end up dating the same man over and over again in different sizes, shapes, and colors until we choose to break the cycle by yielding to God's instructions.

Read the Warning Signs

We ignore all of the warning signs. He is quick-tempered, doesn't keep his promises, has issues with his mother, and on and on. God reveals these things to save us heartache, yet we fail to be alert, so desperate is our heart's cry for someone to love us. We press past the One who loves us most to leap into the arms of someone who has discerned our naivete. And God grieves over us as He looks down the road to see what's coming. So don't be silly, women. Walk in prudence. Exercise discretion. Use discernment. Guard your affections. For they influence everything else in your life (Proverbs 5:23). Exercise good judgment. Accumulate knowledge. Get an understanding of what—and whom—you are dealing with. Proceed carefully. Be accountable, and reverence and fear the God you serve. Make wisdom your closest confidante.

> "'Now then, my sons [daughters], listen to me;
> blessed are those who keep my ways. Listen to my

instruction and be wise; do not ignore it. Blessed is the man [woman] who listens to me, watching daily at my doors, waiting at my doorway. For whoever finds me finds life and receives favor from the LORD. But whoever fails to find me harms himself [herself]; all who hate me love death'" (Proverbs 8:32-36).

God tells us that if we lack wisdom to ask Him, He will generously give it to us without berating us, and yet His throne is the last place we stop when making decisions. Perhaps we don't trust Him with our desires enough. Our perception of what He wants for our lives is misguided, causing us to conclude that we must secure our own joy. Oh, if only we knew the incredible plans He has for us, perhaps we would hold out a little longer! It is His will that we all experience righteousness, peace, and joy in the Holy Ghost in our lives and relationships, right here, right now. Yet the lack of wisdom derails many.

The old saying "You hurt me the first time, shame on you; you hurt me the second time, shame on me" has some grain of truth to it. Because mistakes do happen, God would like us to learn from them. But this was not His initial plan. God wanted us to learn wisdom from *Him* and make wise decisions based on the understanding that *He* gives. However, this is not always the path that we take. And in those moments His grace is there to meet us.

Recently after I spoke at a conference, a woman approached me. Weeping, she told me that her husband was leaving her. She had never lived a day alone. She had literally gone to this man's house from her parents' house and had been married for over twenty years. She was a good wife, she had done all that she could do, and yet it had not been enough. He had an unfaithful spirit, something she had been too young to discern when she first married him. She was afraid, dismayed, and confused. She didn't know what to do. She needed the wisdom of God. For the wife who stands in dismay as her husband announces he is leaving or is shocked to discover his adulterous behavior, what words can anyone offer in their own understanding? No answer would be the right one at a time like this. In the midst of times when one lacks understanding, we—like Paul, who inquired of the Lord why he had to live with the affliction he suffered—must draw the same conclusion this surrendered apostle uttered.

> "But he said to me, 'My grace is **sufficient** for you, for my power is made perfect in weakness.' Therefore I will boast all the more gladly about my weaknesses, so that Christ's power may rest on me" (2 Corinthians 12:9, emphasis mine).

You may be weak from the battering your heart has received in your circumstance, but still God's wisdom awaits you, giving you the invisible reasons, settling the issues within you, and filling in the spaces that the devastation left gaping. And then He comes bearing the balm of Gilead, pouring the ointment into your wounds, allowing His power to rest on you and strengthen you to hold on. Loving you, whispering words of comfort. Encouraging you to rise and be healed—a little bit older, a little bit stronger, and a whole lot wiser.

Take stock of all that has occurred and write down the key moments.

When did you have an idea that something was wrong? What caused you to realize this?

What was your response?

In hindsight, was it the best response? In light of what you know now, what would you do differently?

What has this situation revealed to you about the other person? About yourself?

What needs make you susceptible to making unwise decisions?

How can these be turned to strengths?

Did you consult God in this matter? At what juncture of the circumstance? What was His word to you? Did you follow His advice?

Did you receive counsel from those around you? Why or why not? Have you been careful to seek counsel that you can trust? Have they been victorious in their own lives as a sound example to you?

What have you learned from this experience?

Has it made you bitter or better? In what way?

If confronted by your offender again, what will your response be?

How do you think God would have you respond? What will that do for you? For His purposes?

Do you feel close to God only when things go well? What does this say about your trust level? How far away or close to God are you now? What steps can you take to draw even closer?

Do you believe that God is able to make something good come out of your situation? What area do you struggle with when you consider this?

Are you willing to give your broken crumbs to God and allow Him to make something out of them that can be used for the good of His kingdom and for the betterment of others? Are you able to see the possibilities at this time? How can your situation be used to the good of others?

What seems impossible to you now? What does God's Word say?

Do you really know how God feels about you? What do you think He thinks of you?

What do you think God desires for you most of all?

In order to move on, in what area are you in need of God's wisdom?

Write a list of the questions that have been burning in your heart and give them to God.

Write down God's answers to you. Meditate on them. Rest in them. Give Him time to act.

will lift up mine eyes unto the hills, from whence cometh my help. My help cometh from the LORD....

Psalm 121:1,2 KJV

9

Embracing the Altar

How do you spell relief? I'll tell you how I spell it: J-E-S-U-S. I can truly relate to David. After the death of his infant son by Bathsheba, David took account of his wrong doings, bravely accepting his punishment for his acts of adultery and murder. But one thing made this king's soul quiver—the thought of God no longer wanting to have a relationship with him. This one thing he could not bear the thought of. He could deal with the country being taken away from him. He could deal with the death of a son, no matter how painful that might be. But he could not deal with being separated from God.

> "Do not cast me from your presence or take your Holy Spirit from me. Restore to me the joy of your salvation and grant me a willing spirit, to sustain me" (Psalm 51:11,12).

David's relationship with God meant more to him than anything else. I was not always able to say that in my own personal journey. I must confess that other men—and even dreams—overshadowed God from time to time in my life. And for every time that I placed someone or something as more important than Him, I experienced the shattering of another idol until I, too, was like David, completely reliant on my Savior, hungering and thirsting after the only One who could fill me the way in which I longed to be filled.

The truth of the matter is, we can hold no person or thing dearer than the supreme Lover of our souls. He is the only faithful One. The One who never lies, who never fails. He is Love personified, and no one can love you better. Allow me to speak to you from my heart for a moment. I have found in my own personal struggles with different heartbreaking circumstances that I was guilty of this one thing in all cases—I dashed out of the protection of my Heavenly Father's arms, turned, and took my heart from His care and gave it to one who was either not qualified to care for it or undiscerning of its worth. But even here I cannot fault my offenders completely, because I myself did not know my own worth. I had not remained at my Father's feet long enough to learn of it. Therefore, I attracted those who saw me as I saw myself. They only mirrored what was in my own heart. That was a difficult pill to swallow and, on that note, I took the time to dissociate myself from any further pursuits of human love and pursue instead the One who I knew loved me most of all.

As I gathered up the broken pieces of my heart and redeposited them back into His hands, a miraculous thing began to occur. I found the love I had been looking for. His heart became my sanctuary. I think back to the days when criminals would run to the church and cling to the altar in search of asylum from those who pursued them. This was considered a legal safe place. It's kind of like when people are in trouble in a foreign country. If they can make it to their country's embassy, they can seek refuge or immunity from the laws of the land they are in. What a fitting example this is of Christ Himself. He is our sanctuary.

> "The name of the LORD is a strong tower; the **righteous run** to it and are safe" (Proverbs 18:10, emphasis mine).

> "The LORD is my rock, my fortress and my deliverer; my God is my rock, in whom I take refuge. He is my **shield** and the horn of my salvation, my stronghold" (Psalm 18:2, emphasis mine).

Now, let's talk about exactly what this means for you. The Lord your God is your rock, immovable and strong, a place where you can stand secure. You can sit on Him, lie on Him. He is able to bear your weight without sinking or breaking beneath the pressure of your cares. He can take whatever you're carrying. He is your fortress. You can literally hide yourself inside of Him. Nothing can penetrate the boundaries of protection He surrounds you with. He will deliver you out of your troubles. He is your shield; any arrows the enemy throws will bounce off Him, unable to break your skin or penetrate your heart. He is a safe place for you, your heart, and all that concerns you. Anything that you leave in His care, He is able to keep.

Since my heart has been securely deposited into the hands of my Savior, I find that I am no longer tossed about as before. Yes, I have suffered disappointments, but I have not been deeply hurt. I have been shaken but not moved.

My heart is shielded by the One who knows how to protect it and keep it safe.

> "He who dwells in the shelter of the Most High will rest in the shadow of the Almighty. I will say of the LORD, 'He is my refuge and my fortress, my God, in whom I trust.'...He will cover you with his feathers, and under his wings you will find refuge; his faithfulness will be your shield and rampart. ...If you make the Most High your dwelling—even the LORD, who is my refuge—then no harm will befall you, no disaster will come near your tent" (Psalm 91:1-3,9,10).

Now, mind you, this does not mean that nothing bad will ever happen to you. What it says is that you will be shielded from the worst of it. I am reminded of a dream I once had where I found myself plunged into deep waters. A hand was pulling me through. All the while I kept repeating, "I can't swim! I can't swim!" And yet I emerged completely whole and dry on the other side of the body of water. As I marveled at the experience, I exclaimed, "Wow! I made it!" I recall another such dream where great waters were rising up and covering buildings in their path, but when they reached the building where I resided, the waters halted and I heard a voice say, "It will not come nigh thee." Yes, the tempest has risen high in my life from time to time, but I have been spared from being overtaken. I am still standing in spite of all that has come my way because I have chosen to hide myself in Him. We can all make it if the Lord is our sanctuary. The storms of life may batter the tent from without, but they will not penetrate and destroy the inner contents.

God has admonished us to guard our hearts with all diligence because the issues of life and death will be settled by the decisions we make from the seat of our emotions. If you find yourself unable to be a worthy sentry of this, your most precious charge, give it over to the One who is well able to keep it. Commit your heart to Him daily for His safekeeping.

Why should you trust Him more than any other when others have failed you? Please do not project human frailties onto the only Perfect One in all of creation. Consider His word and embrace it as His personal pledge to you. First of all, He promises that He will never leave you or forsake you. Yes, beloved, He has loved you with an everlasting love from eternity to eternity. Before you were formed in your mother's womb, He knew you and loved you. He made plans for you. He gave Himself for you before you were even aware of who He was!

> "'As the Father has **loved** me, so have I **loved you**.
> Now remain in my love'" (John 15:9, emphasis
> mine).

He loves you, and He invites you to come and hide yourself in His love, to walk in the knowledge that you are loved. You are not alone. No matter who else has left you, there is One who remains.

> "...God has said, 'Never will I **leave** you; never will
> I **forsake** you'" (Hebrews 13:5, emphasis mine).

Promises, Promises

These are the things that you must cling to late in the midnight hour when loneliness overtakes you; in the middle of the afternoon, when sadness assaults you; when you witness others who seem so joyfully unaware of your pain, so caught up are they in their own joy. This is when you meditate on the love notes that He has written to you in His Word.

> "Fix these words of mine in your hearts and minds; tie them as symbols on your hands and bind them on your foreheads" (Deuteronomy 11:18).

> "Bind them upon your heart forever; fasten them around your neck. When you walk, they will guide you; when you sleep, they will watch over you; when you awake, they will speak to you" (Proverbs 6:21,22).

Keep God's promises before you at all times. Meditate on them constantly. Let them guide all that you set your hands to do and let them redirect your thoughts back to what is true, noble, right, pure, lovely, admirable, excellent, and praiseworthy (Philippians 4:8). As Solomon encouraged his son to heed the commands of his father and the instruction of his mother in the book of Proverbs, the same promise applies to the promises our Heavenly Father gives to us. His promises will guide us as we walk through life. They will saturate our dreams and renew our minds. We will wake to find our hearts a little lighter, our lives transforming before our eyes. In our waking moments, the Holy Spirit will bring His sweet promises back to our remembrance should we begin to sag a little toward the middle of the day. He will gently remind us, "Hey, don't forget that you are loved. You have a faithful lover. He renews His mercies toward you every day." Now, that is awesome! He doesn't serve up leftovers; He gives us a fresh pledge of faithfulness every day. It's like having a ceremony to renew your marriage every morning. His love doesn't get stale because He loves us all over again the way He first loved us. And He loves us this way *every single day.*

Get ahold of this because it will bless you. You know that human love gets old. You have to find ways to light a fire under it every now and then to renew the romance. But our Heavenly Bridegroom will never sing "The thrill is gone" to us. Instead He croons, "Every day is like the first time…" Wow! Can you imagine? Having someone in your life who is as passionately in love with you as he was in the beginning, every day, no matter what you looked like, did, or said? Now, that is some kind of love! Andraé Crouch sang, "I don't know why Jesus loves me." Danniebelle Hall sang, "What kind of love is this He has bestowed on me?" and went on to conclude in the chorus that when she saw God and finally knew Him for all that He was, then "I can tell you how this love can be." It is a mystery. But the knowledge of His matchless and immovable love for us is a sanctuary in which we can hide our hurting hearts.

Let's see, He will never lie to you. He won't change His mind in midstream and decide that you are not the one for Him. He is not fickle. His mind is made up about you. He will always be for you and you for Him. He knows you intimately right down to the number of hairs on your head, and His thoughts about you outnumber the grains of sand upon the earth. You are constantly on His mind! Isn't that what you've always wanted to hear from someone whom you loved?

He will give you good things. He longs to bless you over and over again. His intentions toward you are for good and not for calamity. The gifts He gives won't come with sorrow attached to them, only with so many good feelings that you will simply have to give Him praise.

> "Praise the Lord, O my soul, and forget not all his benefits—who forgives all your sins and heals all your diseases, who redeems your life from the pit and crowns you with love and compassion, who satisfies your desires with good things so that your youth is renewed like the eagle's" (Psalm 103:2-5).

Though He desires your praise and worship, He is not consumed by what you can do for Him. He is always mindful of your desires. His love for you is regenerative. The more He pours Himself out upon you and lavishes you with the things he knows you long for, the more you find yourself strengthened by His loving demonstrations. A glow of assurance lights your eyes and puts a spring in your step. Your entire countenance beams with the fulfillment you feel from His love once you release yourself to embrace it. Others will notice the difference and take note.

Out of the Frying Pan

I'll tell you what else this new confidence will do for you. It will keep the wolves at bay. Trust me, they can always sense easy prey. But when they know a kill won't be easy, they keep right on trucking. Don't feel bad when this happens. Remember man's rejection is God's protection. A friend of mine and I were discussing this thought one day and he laughingly said, "Think of all the little fish that get thrown back into the lake because they are too small. They're probably thinking they want to go where the big fish are going. Little do they know they are heading for the frying pan!" You never know what you may be getting saved from. But God knows. Thank Him for delivering you from unforeseen dangers. Don't consider yourself left out in the cold when these things occur. You are more kept than you know. This causes me to recall a Coca-Cola commercial I saw some time back. A young man was trying to rap to a young lady. She, on the other hand, was having none of his entreaties. She very confidently put her hand on her hip and said, "I already got a man." Well, I'm here to tell you, there's something to be said about knowing that you belong to someone, that you are already a prized possession. No matter what anyone else does to you, you know that you are precious to someone.

In spite of your hurt and disappointment, you have to know that "you got a man." And He's got you. You are not displaced and rejected. You are not unloved. You are not an orphan, unwanted and cast aside. "You got a man," a Man who anticipated this time in your life and prepared for it with special words of comfort.

> "No longer will they call you Deserted, or name your land Desolate. But you will be called Heph-zibah, and your land Beulah; for the LORD will take delight in you, and your land will be married. ...and you will be called Sought After, the City No Longer Deserted" (Isaiah 62:4,12).

Why? Because the Lord Himself will come and take up residence in you, filling all the empty places in your soul. He will not view you as used goods. He will not find you undesirable, no matter what you've been through. He will look upon you with eyes of compassion, clear of judgment, and offer you a drink to soothe your parched spirit. Like He did with the Samaritan woman at the well who'd had her share of men—other women's husbands— He will simply offer you cleansing and a better way. Like He did with the woman who was caught in the act of adultery, heartbroken by her shame in front of the masses, He will offer unconditional forgiveness and a chance to begin again. He will ask no questions because He already knows the answers. He has already been witness to all of your struggles. He knows your needs, your vulnerabilities, your every mistake, your every failing, even your naivete. He feels your longing for love and longs to answer it with Himself.

One night I had a dream. You may be saying, *here she goes again with her dreams.* But hey, what can I say? God deals with me in dreams! I entered a place that was like a bathing house, and I stripped to enter one of the shower stalls. A beautiful man entered the shower just as I turned to stand under the faucet. Instantly I knew that this man was someone I could truly love, but I was ashamed because I had scars all over my body. I thought to myself, "Oh, he couldn't love me. He won't like my body; it is too unsightly." But he came toward me, and as I hung my head and refused to meet his gaze so that I could not view his rejection of me, he came and stood behind me and began to gently touch each scar. His touch was so light and so soothing that I began to weep. He never said a word. He never asked me where I got all of those ugly scars. He just took a huge white towel, wrapped me in it, and drew me to himself. When I woke up I was still weeping. I knew the man was Jesus. And He loved me unconditionally, scars and all. He loves you, scars and all, no matter what your history.

The man at the pool of Bethesda had been paralyzed for thirty-eight years and longed to be healed. When Jesus happened by and asked him if he wanted to be healed, he replied, "I have no man to help me down into the pool." Jesus said to him, "Get up! Take up your mat and walk."

The lame man learned that healing was not in the hands of a man, but in the word of the living God. So I say to you, get up! It's true that you have no man to help you to the place of healing. You have something more powerful, more lasting—the word of God and the love of the One who loves you eternally. So get up! Rise and be healed in the name of Jesus!

Do you feel isolated and alone? Can you explain the void you feel?

What natural forms of comfort have you sought? Have they been effective?

Why have you hesitated to go to God?

If God were to sit in front of you right now, what would
you say to Him?

Do you believe He hears you? Why or why not?

What would you like for Him to say to you right now?

Do you struggle with making God your first love? Why?
What are the obstacles for you?

Who consumes most of your thoughts? What are those thoughts driven by?

Does the thought of God's love give you comfort?

Make a list of what He has been to you.

Make a list of the promises you need to hear from Him now. Find a corresponding Scripture that you can cling to as a confirmation from Him.

Make a list of the other trials He's brought you through. What did you learn after each one?

What did you learn about yourself? What did you learn about God?

Do you believe He really loves you? What does that mean to you? What does that say about your worth?

In light of how God sees you, how will you proceed with those who enter your life?

Write down every lie the enemy has ever whispered in your ear about you, then declare it untrue and discard it.

Write down a list of the things that God says about you and attach a Scripture that you can personalize about each one.

Say a prayer to God. Recommit yourself back into His care and then thank Him for His faithfulness toward you.

$\mathscr{D}$o not be afraid; you will not suffer shame. Do not fear disgrace; you will not be humiliated. You will forget the shame of your youth and remember no more the reproach of your widowhood. For your Maker is your husband—the LORD Almighty is his name—the Holy One of Israel is your Redeemer; he is called the God of all the earth.

Isaiah 54:4,5

10

Facing Tomorrow

lright, now that we've been through all the steps, talked about the situation, sorted it all out in theory, here's the difficult part—putting everything you've learned and processed into action. Uh-huh—walking it out. So what do you plan to do with the rest of your life? Tomorrow can sound almost ominous in the aftermath of heartbreak. Sometimes tomorrow doesn't look so bad. Other days tomorrow appears almost cruel and threatening. How many tomorrows can you stand before you cave in? Yesterday you did rather well. You even laughed out loud for the first time in what seems like a long time. Today you're feeling so-so. Tomorrow? You'd rather not think that far ahead. Well, girlfriend, you've got some decisions to make.

Yes, tomorrow is up to you. How it plays out is in your hands. This day decides how your tomorrows will go.

What will you do? Will you work on healing your heart and sealing off the edges so that it never opens again? Have you vowed to never let anyone get that close to you any time soon? Never take that much of your energy? Your love? Your caring? Or will you trust God to keep what you have committed to Him? These are important questions to ask because their answers will affect your joy level.

Some of you are singing, "I'm never gonna fall in love again." You may be looking at your tired, old, wrung-out, dried-up heart and having the same conversation with the Lord that He had with the prophet Ezekiel.

> "The hand of the LORD was upon me, and he brought me out by the Spirit of the LORD and set me in the middle of a valley; it was full of bones. He led me back and forth among them, and I saw a great many bones on the floor of the valley, bones that were very dry. He asked me, 'Son of man, can these bones live?' I said, 'O Sovereign LORD, you alone know.' Then he said to me, 'Prophesy to these bones and say to them, "Dry bones, hear the word of the LORD! This is what the Sovereign LORD says to these bones: I will make breath enter you, and you will come to life…"'
> …Then he said to me: 'Son of man, these bones are the whole house of Israel. They say, "Our bones are dried up and our hope is gone; we are cut off." Therefore prophesy and say to them: "This is what the Sovereign LORD says: O my people, I am going to open your graves and bring you up from them; I will bring you back to the land of Israel. Then you, my people, will know that I am the LORD, when I open your graves and bring you

up from them. I will put my Spirit in you and you will live, and I will settle you in your own land. Then you will know that I the LORD have spoken, and I have done it, declares the LORD"'" (Ezekiel 37:1-5, 11-14).

You might feel that your dreams, your hope of love, your desire for the restoration of your children or your marriage might be dead—dry bones. You might have even convinced yourself that it's alright that way. You've made peace with yourself about it, and you're beginning to get on with your life. But still, every time a small reminder comes up or another chance at love appears, your chest tightens. Trepidation causes your pulse to race. Fear begins to rise. You find yourself sabotaging your new chances in order to control any possibility of disappointment. But notice that it was God who looked at the dry bones and decreed that they should live. He declared that He would be the one to breathe life back into them, to dress them with tendons, muscles, and skin. He would give them the strength to be a strong army again. All would be done by His hand; therefore, all the credit would be His.

The Cycle of Love

Now, don't miss this part. Not only will He bring you back to life, but He will put you in your right place and establish you there. Sometimes the things we cling to become idols and God allows what He must in order to get our attention back on Him as our first love. He doesn't do this because He's mean and ornery but simply because He deserves first place in your heart. Not only does He deserve it, but it's the safest place for you. He will allow all else to die in order to glorify Himself and strengthen you for what lies ahead. Whitney Houston sang a song that asked, "Where do broken hearts go?" She concluded that they return to the open arms of the one who has been waiting for them. How true! God waits for our hearts to come full circle back to Him. This is the cycle of our lives—everything begins and ends with Him.

I think again of the Shunammite woman in 2 Kings 4. Let's look at her experience in more depth than we did in chapter one. If you will allow me to relate my take on the Scriptures, the story goes that she was a prominent woman in the city. One day when Elisha the prophet was passing by, she urged him to join her for dinner. From that time on, Elisha always stopped at her house when he passed that way. The woman finally told her husband that she had perceived Elisha to be a holy man of God and suggested that they build a little room on top of their house to accommodate him when he came to visit. Elisha took note of this and asked the woman what he could do for her because she had been so kind to him. She answered that she was perfectly content and secure and had need of nothing.

But Elisha was not satisfied with the woman's answer. He was determined to give her something to show his appreciation. His servant mentioned that the woman didn't have any children. On that note, Elisha called the woman back and told her she would have a son at approximately that time next year. The woman said, "Don't lie to me!" But sure enough, true to the word of the prophet, she had a son at that time the next year. All was well for a short time, but then one day the little boy complained of a headache. His father sent him home from the fields to his mother and at noon the boy died. The mother got up, put her dead son on the bed in the prophet's room, and asked her husband for a horse so she could go and see the prophet. Her husband asked her if anything was wrong. Why was she going to see the prophet when it was not a religious holiday? She simply answered, "It shall be well."

When the prophet saw her coming in the distance, he sent his servant to ask her if her husband, her child, and herself were well, and still she said, "All is well." But when she came before the prophet, she fell at his feet and asked him,

> "'Did I ask you for a son, my lord?' she said. 'Didn't I tell you, "Don't raise my hopes?"'" (2 Kings 4:28).

Can you relate? Elisha then gave his staff to Gehazi his servant and told him to go and lay the staff on the boy's face. But the Shunammite woman was not satisfied with that at all. She told Elisha she was not leaving without him. So Elisha followed her home and went up to the room, where he prayed, breathed into the boy, got up, walked through the house, came back, and ministered to the boy again, and the child came back to life. He called for the woman to come for her son. She entered the room, prostrated herself before Elisha, then took her son and left the room.

Now, what is the point of all of this? I had to tell you all the details because this is where every woman is at some point in her life. If you're not there now, one day you will be. On the outside you look as if you need nothing, just like the Shunammite woman looked. You've got it all together. Your life looks tidy enough, but deep inside you have a longing that is taking so long to manifest itself that you have decided to forget about it and just make the best of your lot in life. You've invited Jesus in to dine with you, and every now and then He passes by and you share a meal. You know who He is. You recognize that He is someone significant whom you should associate with, avail yourself to, and even serve. You're busy at church or serving others as you think He would have you do. And one day He touches that place in you that you've buried deep inside of yourself and makes you a promise to fulfill the desire of your heart. You draw back. You don't even want Him to awaken what you've put to sleep. Is it some cruel joke? Is it the devil, or is it God? Or is it you wishing one last time? So, you chide yourself to tuck that longing away.

But miraculously one day the thing that God spoke into your spirit has manifested itself right before your very eyes. Can you imagine the Shunammite woman's joy to finally have a son? How she must have loved him and lavished on him to make up for all the years she longed to have this little one in her arms! Perhaps her service to the prophet had fallen off a little as she dealt with her new responsibilities. I find it interesting that her husband found it unusual that she wanted to see the prophet on a day other than a religious occasion. Had she fallen from relationship to religion? But she wasted no time getting back on track.

Going to the Source

She laid her son on the prophet's bed. She revisited the place of the initial promise. She was not going to let the enemy come and steal the word that had been given to her. No, no. She got on her horse. She didn't stop to discuss it with her mother, her friends, or even her husband. She wouldn't even confess that her son was dead. Instead she declared, "It shall be well." I've got to tell you, I think the woman was a sister! I can just see her mumbling under her breath as she rode that donkey as hard and fast as she could, "Oh, no, you spoke that child into this world, you're going to speak him back. I didn't ask for him, but now that I've got him I'm not giving him up that easy. You've got to fix this thing!" She didn't have time to talk to anyone who couldn't do something about her situation. Mm-mm.

She didn't have time to fool around with even Elisha's servant. She wasn't interested in any remedies that he possessed. She was going straight to the source, to the one who had spoken her child into existence. He was the only one who could breathe life back into his cold bones. But here is what I find interesting. After all this anxiety, when Elisha brings the boy back to life and he calls for his mother, the Shunammite woman doesn't reach for her son first. She falls at the feet of Elisha in a show of gratitude before taking hold of her son.

This, my sisters, is the moral of the story. A friend of mine asked me, "Why did God allow the child to die?" My answer was, "I find it interesting that you stopped at the child's death and didn't keep going to his resurrection." So many of us stop in the middle of our trial and settle for comfort, which is represented by the staff Gehazi laid on the child's face unsuccessfully trying to revive him. Don't settle for comfort in your situation. Press in for the miracle. Refuse to let go of the feet of Jesus until He blesses you, until He either brings your marriage back to life, your dreams into manifestation, or makes true love a reality to you. Whatever your dead situation is that makes you wonder if your dry heart can live again, declare, "It shall be well," and go in pursuit of Him. This is not the time to collect opinions along the way. Chart your course straight for His throne room and don't stop until you get there. You see, others will help you bury your situation before God is able to redeem it and glorify Himself in your midst. However, there is only one word of caution: Examine your motive for why you are clinging to what you believe to be the promise. James 4:2,3 says, "You do not have, because you do not ask God. When you ask, you do not receive, because you ask with wrong motives."

Make sure the promises are of God and not simply a desire of your own flesh. Remember, He says, "Though [the promise] tarry, wait for it" (Habakkuk 2:3 KJV). Don't get discouraged by the passage of time. If it is of God, peace will accompany the promise and it will truly come to pass. But if it is of the flesh, it will lead you to disappointment.

Which raises the point that you must also understand and know, that God allowed the child to die for the same reason He allows anything in our lives to die—to get our attention back on Him. To realign our priorities. To cause us to realize and understand that we can't get too caught up in the stuff, the people, the situations, that we hold so dear. Let us not get lost in worshipping the gift and lose sight of the Giver, or become restrained and religious with Him while we lavish our hearts on our desire, only acknowledging Him according to habit or obligation.

You can trust Him to back you up and get you to start over, so deep is His love for you. He won't allow you to wander farther and farther away from His presence, seeking Him less and less until He's forced to wait for Sunday for a visit from you. No, He will allow something in your world to die, and then He will come when you call, bringing His healing with Him, once again walking through every room in the house of your heart. You see, He won't be assigned to one room. He wants them all. And then He will breathe life back into your heart. Back into your home. Back into your relationships, your dreams, your cherished spaces. But this time you will keep sight of what is truly important and, before you clasp the gift of restoration that He holds out to you, you will bow and worship Him.

So perhaps you feel that you've buttoned up the hatches of your heart. You've spoken to yourself and said, "That's alright, I don't really need a man. I don't need anyone. I can make it on my own." Trust me, God knows better.

> "And he who **searches** our hearts knows the mind of the **Spirit**, because the **Spirit** intercedes for the saints in accordance with God's will" (Romans 8:27, emphasis mine).

The Holy Spirit will expose your unspoken longings to God, and when God has taken notice of your service to Him, He will come bringing His promises to you, delivering the desires of your heart you thought He hadn't taken notice of. And it will happen when you least expect it, when you are lost in service to Him. You see, the Shunammite woman recognized Elisha as a man of God and had turned all of her attention to serving him. This is what started the whole thing. God decided it was time to bless her. As you come into the fullness of who God is, what He is to you, and the place He deserves in your life, you will begin to serve Him wholeheartedly, and He will decide to bless you—completely unsolicited.

> "Delight yourself in the LORD and he will give you the **desires** of your **heart**" (Psalm 37:4, emphasis mine).

I used to hate that Scripture. I wanted what I wanted, when I wanted it. But the more I got rid of myself and filled myself with His love for me, the less I became sure of what I really wanted. This freed God to begin to fill my life with pleasant surprises. I found that He knew the desires of my heart even better than I did! Do I have *every* single thing that I want right now? No. But I truly have enough. Do I have a man in my life? No and yes. I do not have a man in the flesh, but I do have a true Lover of my soul, One who fills me up from the inside out. Have I had my share of pain, disappointment, and heartbreak? Oh, yes, indeed! But there are no dry bones present at my house. Definitely, beyond the shadow of a doubt, *all is well*.

Will you live? Yes, my sweet. Will you love again? For every time I've uttered that I won't, I've done it again and found it sweeter than the last time. If you are living and breathing, you most definitely will love again. It is inevitable because Love Himself resides inside of you.

"We love because he first loved us" (1 John 4:19).

There is no way that you can keep all that love to yourself. You've got to share the wealth. Will you be more discerning next go round? That's up to you. But for now, until you are truly feeling it all the way down to your bones, I suggest that you set off in search of a deeper, more intimate relationship with the One who loves you passionately and eternally, all the while proclaiming to the wind and anyone who will listen that, "All is well."

"I will betroth you to me forever; I will betroth you in righteousness and justice, in love and compassion. I will betroth you in faithfulness, and you will acknowledge the LORD" (Hosea 2:19,20).

What areas of your life would you consider to be dry? Not able to be revived?

Do you believe that God is able to breathe life back into those dead places?

Are you willing to allow God to do the reviving? Will you allow Him to set you in the right place? Are you willing to surrender where you think that place should be?

Have you managed to perfect an image for yourself that covers your needs and longings?

Do you still pray about them, or have you given up? Why? What is God's truth versus how you feel?

What vows or decisions have you made about your future?

Do you look forward to embracing love again? What is your outlook on love?

Are you afraid of the possibility of being hurt again? Why? Do you anticipate being hurt again? What reinforces your fear of repeated heartbreak? What godly steps can you take to prevent this from happening?

Do you trust God to keep your heart? How will you cooperate with Him?

What desires have you tucked away? Why do you struggle with believing that God will give you your longings?

Are you choosing to delight yourself in Him until He brings your desires to pass? How are you making accommodation for the Lord in the house of your life?

In what way are you serving Him and seeking to please Him? Do you feel His regard as you apply yourself to waiting on Him?

When someone brings up the things that you secretly desire, what is your reaction? Why?

Can you keep God first after you have received your desire? How will you keep your priorities in focus?

Are you presently in relationship with the Lord or merely religious? What is the difference?

Be honest about the conditions you held God to in exchange for your love. How do you feel about God when things don't go the way you wanted them to? How do you feel when He allows you to lose the things you hold dear?

Is it His right to remove things that He knows are not good for you? That stand between yourself and Him? What has He sacrificed for your sake? Have you sacrificed as much?

After all that He has done for you, what does He deserve from you? What can you do to please His heart? What will He do in return according to His word?

What are His promises of love to you? Do a word search in the Scriptures on the words "love" and "faithfulness." Write them down and personalize them to yourself.

Write a new love covenant between yourself and the Lord right now. Write down every idol you are discarding from your life and your heart. Sacrifice back to Him anything that has replaced your love for Him, and begin again.

$\mathcal{I}$ will not leave you **comfortless**: I will come to you.

John 14:18 KJV, emphasis mine

Other Books by
Michelle McKinney Hammond

What to Do Until Love Finds You
Secrets of an Irresistible Woman
His Love Always Finds Me
The Power of Femininity
Get a Love Life
If Men Are Like Buses, Then How Do I Catch One?
Prayer Guide for the Brokenhearted

Recommended Reading

Prayer Guide for the Brokenhearted
by Michelle McKinney Hammond

Woman, Thou Art Loosed!
by T.D. Jakes

The Lady, Her Lover & Her Lord
by T.D. Jakes

Betrayal's Baby
by P.B. Wilson

When Forgiveness Doesn't Make Sense
by Robert Jeffress

The Divine Romance
by Gene Edwards

Come Away, My Beloved
by Frances J. Roberts

Heart Hunger
by Cindi McMenamin

Blessed Are the Desperate for They Will Find Hope
by Bonnie Keen

Ladies, be as determined to get information as you are to embrace anything that is important to you. If your local bookstores do not have these books in stock, they are always happy to order them for you. When all else fails, there's always Amazon.com. Happy reading, and stay blessed by the power that acquiring His wisdom brings!

To correspond with Ms. McKinney Hammond,
please write to:

HeartWing Ministries
P.O. Box 11052
Chicago, IL 60611

Or email her at:

mmhammond@mindspring.com

For speaking engagement inquiries, contact:

Speak Up Speaker Services
1-810-982-0898